Calicoes & Quilts
Unlimited

*Nancy -
Please enjoy!
Judy*

Judy Betts Morrison

Gold Fever

Credits

Technical Editor .... Ursula Reikes
Editorial Director .... Kerry I. Hoffman
Managing Editor .... Greg Sharp
Design Director .... Judy Petry
Text and Cover Designer .... Cheryl Stevenson
Production Assistant .... Dani Ritchardson
Illustrators .... Carolyn Kraft
                                                      Laurel Strand
Illustration Assistant .... Bruce Stout
Copy Editor .... Tina Cook
Proofreader .... Melissa Riesland
Photographer .... Brent Kane

Calicoes & Quilts Unlimited
© 1996 by Judy Betts Morrison
That Patchwork Place, Inc., PO Box 118
Bothell, WA 98041-0118 USA

Printed in the United States of America
01 00 99 98 97 96   6 5 4 3 2 1

Library of Congress Cataloging-in-Publication Data

Morrison, Judy Betts,
    Calicoes & Quilts Unlimited / Judy Betts Morrison.
        p. cm. — (New American quilt shop series)
    ISBN 1-56477-140-7
    1. Patchwork—Patterns. 2. Quilting—Patterns. 3. Appliqué—Pat-
terns. 4. Calicoes & Quilts Unlimited. I. Title. II. Series.
TT835.M689 1996
746.46'041—dc20   96-13764
                                                          CIP

MISSION STATEMENT

We are dedicated to providing quality products and services that inspire creativity. We work together to enrich the lives we touch.

That Patchwork Place is a financially responsible ESOP company.

Greetings from Alaska

Dedication

This book is dedicated to:

My husband, Tom, for standing beside me for the past twenty-nine years saying, "You can do it, Judith," and for picking up the slack around the house while I was married to my computer.

My son, Michael, who creates smiles and laughter.

My mother, Jackie Grow, who has shared her creative genes, humor, and work ethic.

Acknowledgments

Thanks to:

That Patchwork Place and Kerry Hoffman, for offering this opportunity to show our Alaskan quilters to the world.

My talented staff and teachers: Jeanie Smith, Ann Hartig Corkran, Clara Limberg, Dee Morrow, Jean Campbell, Kathy Mosher, and friends Ramona Chinn, Carol Johnson, and George Taylor, who have all shared their ideas and efforts unselfishly throughout this project. Without their dedication and help, this book would not have been possible. You are all champions in my book!

Judy Hopkins, who so graciously answered all my many questions, for sharing her text from Down the Rotary Road with Judy Hopkins so I wouldn't have to reinvent the wheel, and for contributing a quilt to my book so I would have a "famous author" represented.

Jean Campbell, for sharing her technique of raw-edge dimensional appliqué.

Trish Stewart, who developed a shirt design that shows off Alaskan animals in cartoon characters and the many quilts in this book.

Doug Nolte, for keeping my wheels rolling and my driveway plowed.

North to
Alaska

Contents

Meet Judy Betts Morrison

I am a third-generation Alaskan and very proud of the strong-willed, adventurous women in my family. The words "can't do" are not a part of our vocabulary. You do what needs to be done to get on with your life.

I was raised in the Matanuska Valley, along with three sisters and two brothers, and was eighteen years old when I made my first trip outside Alaska to attend Kinman Business School in Spokane, Washington. After graduation, I moved to Anchorage (where I was born) and have lived here for more than thirty years.

I opened Calicoes & Quilts Unlimited in June 1982 because I wanted to be in the quilting business. Having never worked in retail, I had no idea what I was committing my family or finances to; however, we had

just sold another business, and my husband said, "Go for it!" I am still grateful that we did. My son, Michael (now 18 and off to college), was five and just entering kindergarten when we opened. When he was a youngster and not feeling well, I would bring him to the shop with his favorite pillow and quilts and let him sleep under the classroom tables. Michael continues to push my button about Calicoes & Quilts not being work because I'm just doing my hobby! Needless to say, both of my men appreciate the work and effort it takes to run a small business.

I have always loved working with my hands, and I enjoy teaching and being with the customers. Through the years, I have attended quilting classes with local and national quilt teachers at various quilt conferences and seminars. This past year has been a benchmark for me since I have now worked longer for myself than I did for the Federal Aviation Administration, where I gained the expertise for working with others.

My mother, Jackie Grow, presently lives in the Matanuska Valley a few miles north of Palmer. Her picturesque log home, set against mountains, barns, and a vegetable garden, was built in 1935 and is listed in the National Historic Register as an original colonist home. She lived in eight different small towns throughout Alaska before marrying my stepfather, Dave Grow. Once she bought her dream house, Mom vowed she would not move again. That was thirty-eight years ago, and she has stayed put. She is a

At left, Judy Betts Morrison. At right, clockwise: Judy's parents, Jackie Grow and Thur Betts, 1941. Jackie Grow and Judy's grandmother, Clara Slumberger, 1938. The author and Archie, 1954.

woman of her word. My mother is still my main teacher—we spend many wonderful hours creating marvelous handcrafted items and enjoying each other's company.

My grandmother, Clara Slumberger, came to Alaska in 1920 as a schoolteacher for the Territory of Alaska. My mother would have been born in Alaska except that Grandma wanted to be with her mother in Washington state. When only six months old, my mother made her first of many trips to and from Alaska on a steamship, which was then a standard form of travel. Grandma taught in southeastern and southcentral Alaska in six different Alaskan communities, living above or behind the schools, as well as in Washington state. Both she and my mother are true Alaska pioneers.

Calicoes & Quilts Unlimited

Calicoes & Quilts Unlimited (also known as "The Shop") is located at the base of the Chugach Mountains in south Anchorage, a small city of 250,000 people. The Shop is five minutes from my home and the same distance from local schools, which is the main reason why I opened it in an out-of-the-way business park. Over time, businesses have grown up all around us.

The 1,450 square feet of The Shop is packed with more than 1,750 bolts of fabric and all the latest quilting books, patterns, and

notions. Since we were the first to occupy this space, we chose to keep our high ceilings for displaying our class, book, and pattern samples. We built cubicles for the fabric and made special areas where we could hang and stack quilts and battings. We even have a place for children to play!

Calicoes & Quilts Unlimited provides an opportunity for women to be together and sort out the problems of everyday life. Alaska is hard on women. Most are far away from their roots in the lower forty-eight states, and the harsh, cold climate and dark winter days make being away from their loved ones all the more difficult. The Shop provides a safe haven for women, who come to talk, share creative ideas, and get help on their projects. We provide sunshine, smiles, and hugs every day of the year no matter what the weather.

Classes have always been our joy—a chance for women to come together and share their experiences and learn new things. Lasting friendships are often made. We teach classes four nights a week and on Saturday and Sunday. We offer beginner, intermediate, and advanced classes in traditional and nontraditional quilting methods, and we continue to change and grow with our customers.

I hope you enjoy looking at our organized clutter and wonderful quilts!

Employees, teachers, and friends of Calicoes & Quilts Unlimited. Standing, from left: Jeanie Smith, George Taylor, Dee Morrow. Sitting, from left: Kathy Mosher, Ann Hartig Corkran, Jean Campbell, Judy Betts Morrison.

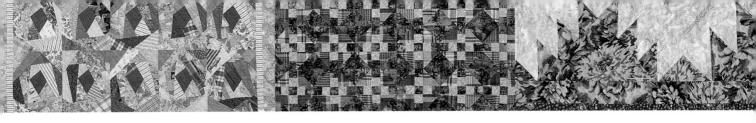

Quilt Patterns

This section contains instructions for making fourteen quilts. Read the complete cutting and piecing directions for the quilt you plan to make, and consult "General Directions" on pages 70–75 before you begin. We have tried to make the instructions clear and simple. You might want to make a sample block before proceeding with the entire quilt to test the pattern and confirm your fabric choices.

The finished quilt dimensions given in the pattern instructions may be larger or smaller than the dimensions given for the quilts in the photo captions. The pattern dimensions are based on unquilted tops that are assumed to have been cut and sewn with absolute precision. The dimensions of the pictured quilts reflect reality—the compounded effects of slight inaccuracies in cutting or piecing, and

any stretching or "take-up" that might have occurred during the quilting process.

The yardage requirements in the materials list should be adequate to complete the project if your fabric was cut evenly from the bolt and does not shrink significantly when prewashed. Yardage calculations are based on 44"-wide fabric that has at least 42" of usable width after preshrinking. If your preshrunk fabric is narrower than 42", you may need additional fabric to cut the required number of pieces. On the other hand, if your fabric is 42" wide or wider and you crosscut to the end of a strip without counting the pieces, you may end up with more pieces than you need to make a particular block or quilt. Save extras for a "leftovers" quilt.

Unless specified otherwise, all cutting dimensions include ¼"-wide seam allowances. Do not add seam allowances to the dimensions given in the cutting instructions.

Cutting specifications for triangles indicate the size of the square from which the triangles will be cut. Directions for half-square triangles instruct you to cut squares "once diagonally," and "twice diagonally" for quarter-square triangles. If you need a refresher, see "Rotary Cutting" on page 70.

We make quick half-square triangle units from layered strips. Detailed instructions for this simple method appear on pages 71–72.

Use the photos and drawings that accompany the patterns as a reference while assembling your blocks and quilt. If you need to square up your blocks before assembling your quilt top, see "Squaring Up Blocks" on page 76. For help with setting your blocks on point, see "On-Point Sets" on page 77.

See "Borders" on pages 78–80 for detailed information about bordering your quilt. Most of the quilts in this book are finished with borders with straight-cut corners. Unless otherwise noted, borders are made from strips cut along the crosswise grain of the fabric and seamed where extra length is needed. Border strips are cut extralong, then trimmed to fit when the actual dimensions of the center section of the quilt are known. Purchase additional fabric if you want to cut strips along the lengthwise grain for unpieced borders.

General information about finishing your quilt—such as marking the quilting lines or adding a sleeve and label—is on pages 80–87.

Blowing in the Wind

Blowing in the Wind *by Judy Betts Morrison and Kathy Mosher, 1995, Anchorage, Alaska, 39" x 39". Machine quilted by Kathy Mosher.*

By Judy Betts Morrison & Kathy Mosher

The Alaska fireweed on a color-wash background of flowers, mountains, and sky depicts Alaska in full bloom. Popular legend holds that our first snow will fall six weeks after the fireweed goes to seed. Kathy and I used a raw-edge dimensional appliqué technique to make the three-dimensional fireweed flowers and leaves.

Color Key

- Yellow prints
- White prints
- Blue prints
- Beige prints
- Gray prints
- Light floral prints
- Light green print

Dimensions: 40½" x 40½"

31½" pieced center; 4¾"-wide border

Materials: 44"-wide fabric

◇ **For the border and binding**
  ¼ yd. *each* of yellow, white, blue, floral, and green prints

◇ **For the background and fireweed**
  ¼ yd. total assorted yellow prints for the sky
  ¼ yd. total assorted white prints for the sky
  ¼ yd. total assorted blue prints for the sky
  ¼ yd. total assorted beige prints for the sky
  ¼ yd. total assorted gray prints for the mountain
  ½ yd. total assorted light floral prints for the wildflower field
  ¼ yd. total assorted pink and fuchsia prints for the fireweed flowers
  ¼ yd. total assorted green prints for the fireweed leaves

◇ **Additional materials**
  1⅓ yds. for backing
  Batting
  1½ yds. fleece for the design wall
  Assorted beads (bugle and seed) for stamens
  Crewel yarn and/or silk ribbon in assorted dark reds for flower stems and buds
  Green DMC perle cotton #8
  3 to 4 bottles Dritz® Fray Check™
  Old paint brush
  Cardboard box lids or cookie sheets

Cutting

◇ **From the prints for the border, cut:**

Fabric	Strip Size	Border Piece
Yellow	5" x 13¼"	9
	5" x 17¾"	6
White	5" x 8⅜"	7
	5" x 11⅜"	8
Blue	5" x 14⅜"	1
	5" x 27⅞"	10
Floral	5" x 17⅜"	5
	5" x 24⅞"	4
Green	5" x 21⅞"	3
	5" x 23⅜"	2

◇ **From the prints for the binding, cut:**

Fabric	Strip Size	Binding Piece
Yellow print	2½" x 15¼"	6
	2½" x 10¾"	9
White print	2½" x 9"	7
	2½" x 9"	8
Blue print	2½" x 16"	1
	2½" x 32"	10
Floral print	2½" x 29"	4
	2½" x 26"	5
Green print	2½" x 32"	2
	2½" x 19"	3

◇ **From the prints for the background, cut the following number of squares, each 2" x 2":**

Assorted yellows	63
Assorted whites	47
Assorted blues	60
Assorted beiges	46
Assorted grays	57
Assorted florals	168

—— Note ——

Cut a few more squares of each color than you need so that you have extras to play with when arranging the background.

———————

Assembling the Background

1. Pin the fleece to a wall. Arrange the 2" squares on the fleece, following the diagram at right. Use the floral prints for the wildflower field, the gray prints for the mountain, and the blue, white, yellow, and beige prints for the sky. Place the light and dark values carefully to make the various areas distinct. Refer to the color photo on page 12 to see how each area is shaded from light to dark. Play with the arrangement until you are satisfied with the design.

o	o	o	o	o	o	o	o	o	o	o	o	y	y	b	y	y	y	y	y
o	o	o	o	o	o	o	o	o	o	o	o	y	y	b	b	y	y	w	y
o	o	o	o	o	o	o	o	o	o	y	y	y	b	y	y	w	w	w	y
o	o	o	o	o	o	o	o	o	y	y	y	b	y	y	w	w	w	w	y
o	o	o	o	o	o	o	o	y	y	b	b	y	y	y	w	w	w	w	y
o	o	o	o	o	b	b	b	y	b	y	y	y	y	y	w	w	w	y	y
o	o	o	o	b	b	b	b	b	y	w	w	w	w	w	w	w	w	y	y
b	o	b	b	b	b	b	b	t	t	t	w	w	w	w	w	w	y	y	b
b	b	b	b	b	b	b	t	t	t	t	t	w	w	w	w	y	y	y	b
t	b	b	b	b	b	t	t	t	t	t	t	t	w	w	w	y	y	b	y
t	t	b	b	b	t	t	t	t	t	t	t	t	t	w	w	w	y	b	y
t	t	t	b	t	t	t	t	t	t	t	t	t	t	t	w	w	b	y	y
t	t	t	t	t	t	t	t	t	t	t	t	t	t	t	t	w	w	w	y
x	x	x	x	x	x	x	x	x	x	x	x	x	x	x	x	x	x	x	x
x	x	x	x	x	x	x	x	x	x	x	x	x	x	x	x	x	x	x	x
x	x	x	x	x	x	x	x	x	x	x	x	x	x	x	x	x	x	x	x
x	x	x	x	x	x	x	x	x	x	x	x	x	x	x	x	x	x	x	x
x	x	x	x	x	x	x	x	x	x	x	x	x	x	x	x	x	x	x	x
x	x	x	x	x	x	x	x	x	x	x	x	x	x	x	x	x	x	x	x
x	x	x	x	x	x	x	x	x	x	x	x	x	x	x	x	x	x	x	x
x	x	x	x	x	x	x	x	x	x	x	x	x	x	x	x	x	x	x	x

y = Yellow prints
w = White prints
o = Blue prints
b = Beige prints
t = Gray prints
x = Floral prints

-- NOTE --

Use a Ruby Beholder® or a reducing glass to view the effects of the fabric placement.

2. Remove one horizontal row of squares at a time from the design wall. Place them in order in a single stack. Sew the squares together, being careful not to get any out of order. Press the seams in opposite directions from row to row. Join the rows. Press the quilt top.

3. Cut the ends of the border strips at a 45° angle as shown. Place the ruler's 45°-angle line along the bottom edge of the strip so that the straight edge of the ruler intersects the corner of the strip. The measurements in the illustrations at right indicate the size of the border piece, including seam allowances.

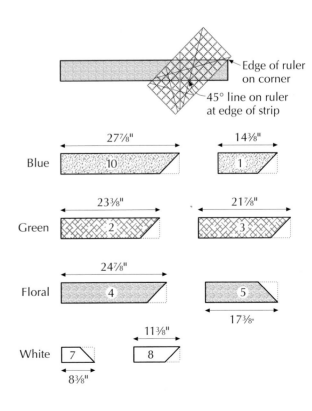

Edge of ruler on corner

45° line on ruler at edge of strip

Blue — 27⅞" — 10 ; 14⅜" — 1

Green — 23⅜" — 2 ; 21⅞" — 3

Floral — 24⅞" — 4 ; 5 — 17⅜"

White — 8⅜" — 7 ; 11⅜" — 8

4. Repeat step 3 to cut both ends of the yellow border strips at a 45° angle as shown.

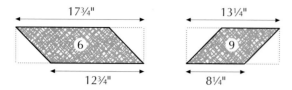

5. Join the border strips for each side with diagonal seams. Sew the border strips to the sides of the quilt top first, then to the top and bottom edges. Try to match the seams in the border strips to the seams in the quilt top.

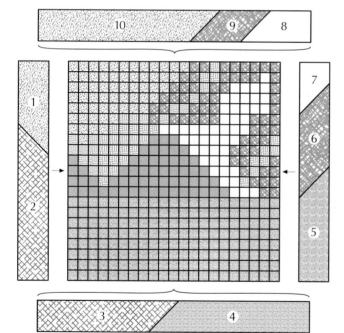

6. Layer the quilt top with batting and backing. Pin-baste together.

7. Machine quilt using monofilament thread on top and cotton thread in the bobbin to match the backing. See quilting suggestion on the opposite page.

8. Cut the ends of the binding strips at a 45° angle as shown. Refer to step 3 on page 15 for cutting directions.

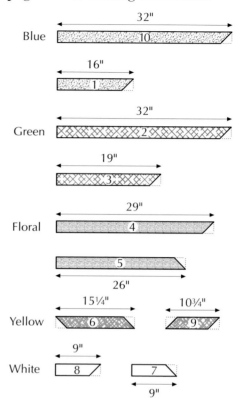

9. Use a diagonal seam to join the binding strips for each side of the quilt. Attach the binding, referring to "Bindings with Measured Strips" on page 86. Try to match the diagonal seams in the binding with the diagonal seams in the borders.

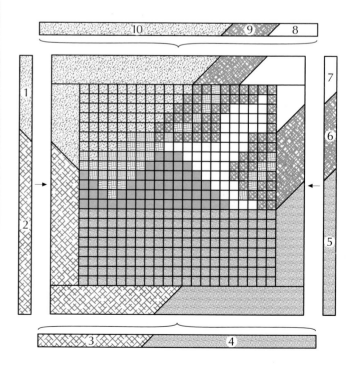

Appliquéing the Fireweed

Use the fireweed templates on pages 90–91.

1. Trace the fireweed templates onto stiff paper and cut out.
2. Cut small pieces of fabric large enough for flowers, flower stems, and leaves. You will need enough assorted pink pieces to cut approximately 42 flowers and 10 stems, and enough assorted green pieces to cut approximately 30 leaves. *Do not cut pattern pieces out yet.*
3. Place the fabric pieces on the cardboard lid or cookie sheet and drip Fray Check on the fabric. Spread quickly using an old brush. Turn the pieces over and re-peat, making sure the fabric is saturated. It is *very important* that the fabric does not sit in one spot for too long, or a film will develop on one side. Wave each piece to air dry. When the fabric is par-tially dry, drape it over the edge of the cardboard lid. Turn the pieces fre-quently until they are dry to avoid creasing the fabric. The Fray Check keeps the fabric from raveling, so there is no need to finish the edges.
4. The fabric will be slightly stiff when com-pletely dry. Lay the templates on top of the fabric. Pin or hold the templates in place and cut around each template using scissors. It is not necessary to trace around the edges before cutting. Referring to the templates, lightly draw lines in the middle of each flower. Cut approximately 42 flowers, 10 stems, and 30 leaves.
5. Arrange the flowers, stems, and leaves on the background and pin in place. Ar-range as shown in the photo on page 12 or create your own design. Add or delete pieces as needed to suit your design.
6. To make the flowers three-dimensional, finger-press small pleats on the lines in the middle of each flower. Attach the flowers to the quilt top with cotton thread, stitching through the center only and securing the pleats. Use green perle cotton to attach the leaves, stitching through the middle of the leaves to create veins. Do not stitch the edges of the flow-ers and leaves to the quilt top. Arrange the stems behind the flowers, tacking only the bottom of the stem with thread.

7. Embroider the flower stalks in a chain stitch using silk ribbon or wool crewel. Embroider the flower buds in a lazy-daisy stitch using silk ribbon. (See "Em-broidery Stitches" on page 75.)
8. Add assorted beads in the middle of each flower for stamens.

9. Label your quilt.

Quilting Suggestion

Alaska Homestead (Variation)

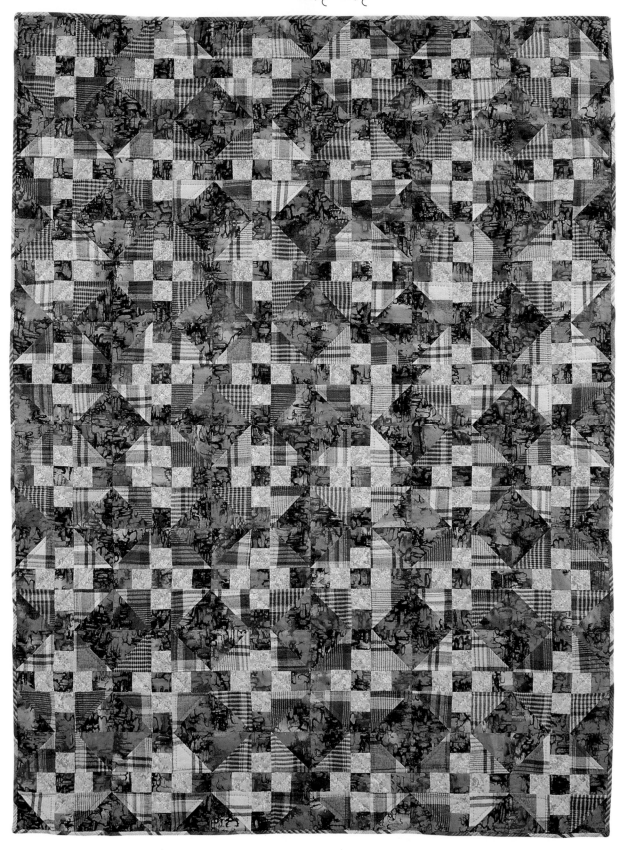

Alaska Homestead (Variation) by *Judy Betts Morrison, 1995, Anchorage, Alaska, 58" x 77". Utility quilted with perle cotton.*

By Judy Betts Morrison

This quilt reminds me of the happy summers I spent as a teenager, riding horses with friends throughout the Matanuska Valley. Color was everywhere—the pinks and fuchsias of the fireweed flowers, the yellow of the buttercups, and the greens of the lush ground cover and trees. I used a flannel plaid and a pink batik to give this quilt texture, and a wool batting for warmth.

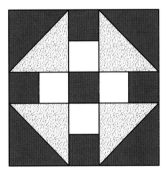

Alaska Homestead
(Variation)

Dimensions: 60" x 80"

48 blocks, 10", set 6 across and 8 down; no border

Materials: 44"-wide fabric

2⅞ yds. dark pink batik
1⅞ yds. flannel plaid for blocks
1 yd. yellow print
½ yd. flannel plaid for 298" of binding
4 yds. for backing (pieced with crosswise seam)
Wool batting
DMC perle cotton #8

— Note —

Flannel yardage includes allowance for shrinkage. If necessary, add more yardage for your particular flannel.

Cutting

◇ *From the pink, cut:*
   15 strips, each 2½" x 42"
   12 strips, each 4⅞" x 42"
◇ *From the plaid for blocks, cut:*
   12 strips, each 4⅞" x 42"
◇ *From the yellow, cut:*
   12 strips, each 2½" x 42"

Directions

1. See "Quick Half-Square Triangle Units" on pages 71–72. Layer the 4⅞"-wide pink and 4⅞"-wide plaid strips right sides together to make a contrasting strip pair. Make 12 strip pairs. Cut the strip pairs into a total of 96 squares, each 4⅞" x 4⅞". Cut the squares once diagonally and chain stitch the resulting triangle pairs along the long edges to make half-square triangle units.

Make 192.

2. Sew a 2½"-wide pink strip to a 2½"-wide yellow strip to make a strip unit. Make 12 strip units. Cut a total of 192 segments, each 2½" wide, from the strip units.

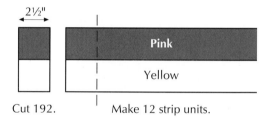

Cut 192.   Make 12 strip units.

3. Cut the 3 remaining 2½"-wide pink strips into a total of 48 squares, each 2½" x 2½". Sew the units together, following the piecing diagram.

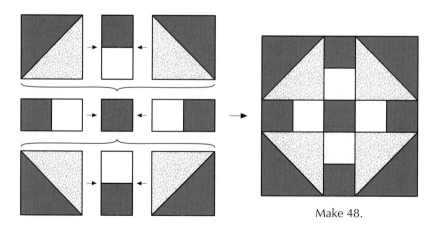

Make 48.

4. Set the blocks together in 8 rows of 6 blocks each. Join the rows.

5. Layer the quilt top with batting and backing; quilt or tie. See the quilting suggestion below. Crow Footing (pages 83–84) was used on the seams between the blocks.

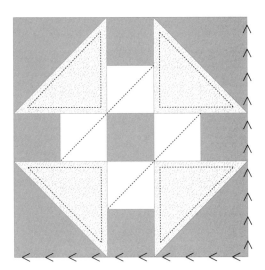

Quilting Suggestion

6. Bind the edges.
7. Label your quilt.

Binky and Friends

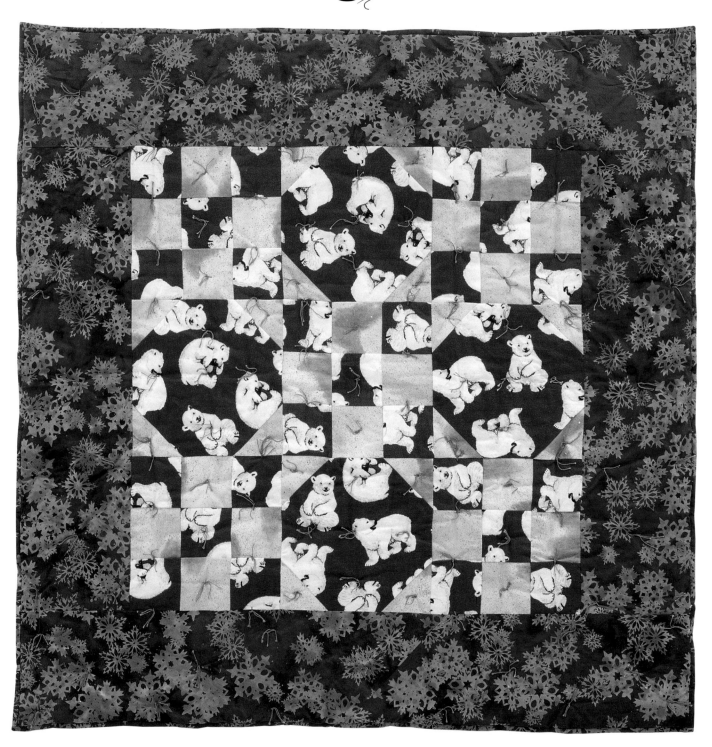

Binky and Friends by Judy Betts Morrison, 1995, Anchorage, Alaska, 46" x 46". Tied with perle cotton by Tom Morrison.

By Judy Betts Morrison

When you think of Alaska, you think of polar bears and snow; therefore, it is only appropriate that we have a quilt with both of them. Flannel and cotton are used in this combination of Nine Patch and Snowball blocks to make a warm and cuddly baby blanket.

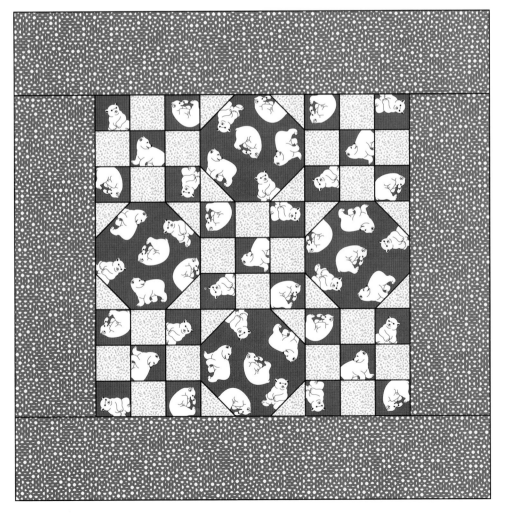

Nine Patch

Snowball

Dimensions: 48" x 48"

5 Nine Patch and 4 Snowball blocks, 10½", set 3 across and 3 down; 8¼"-wide border

Materials: 44"-wide fabric

1⅛ yds. flannel bear print
¾ yd. light blue print
1½ yds. dark blue print for border
3 yds. for backing (or 1½ yds. plus leftovers for a pieced backing)
½ yd. for 216" of binding
Extraloft batting
DMC perle cotton #5 (if you plan to tie the quilt)

---NOTE---

Flannel yardage includes allowance for shrinkage. If necessary, add more yardage for your particular flannel.

Cutting

◇ *From the bear print, cut:*
   3 strips, each 4" x 42"
   2 strips, each 11" x 42"; crosscut into
      4 squares, each 11" x 11"
◇ *From the light blue print, cut:*
   3 strips, each 4" x 42"
   2 strips, each 4⅛" x 42"; crosscut into
      16 squares, each 4⅛" x 4⅛"
◇ *From the dark blue print, cut:*
   4 strips, each 8½" x 42", from the
      lengthwise grain

Directions

1. Sew a bear print strip to each side of a light blue strip to make 1 strip unit. Cut 10 segments, each 4" wide.

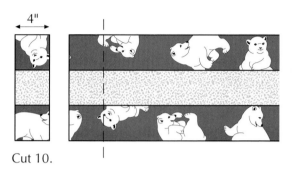

Cut 10.

2. Sew a light blue strip to each side of a bear print strip to make 1 strip unit. Cut 5 segments, each 4" wide.

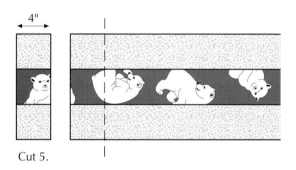

Cut 5.

3. Join the segments to make a Nine Patch block.

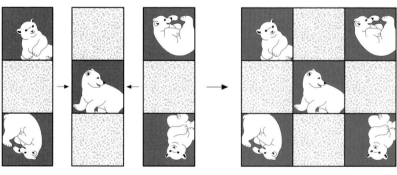

Make 5.

4. Draw a diagonal line on the wrong side of the 4⅛" light blue squares. Place the blue squares on the corners of the 11" bear print squares, arranging the drawn lines as shown.

5. Stitch on the drawn lines, then trim the excess fabric ¼" from the stitching line. Press the seams toward the light blue triangles.

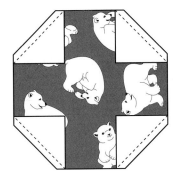

Make 4.

6. Set the blocks together in 3 rows of 3 blocks each, alternating the blocks as shown in the quilt plan on page 23. Join the rows.
7. Add the 8½"-wide border strips to the sides first, then to the top and bottom edges. See "Straight-Cut Corners" on pages 78–79.
8. Layer the quilt top with batting and backing. Tie with perle cotton about every 4".
9. Bind the edges.
10. Label your quilt.

Cabin Fever

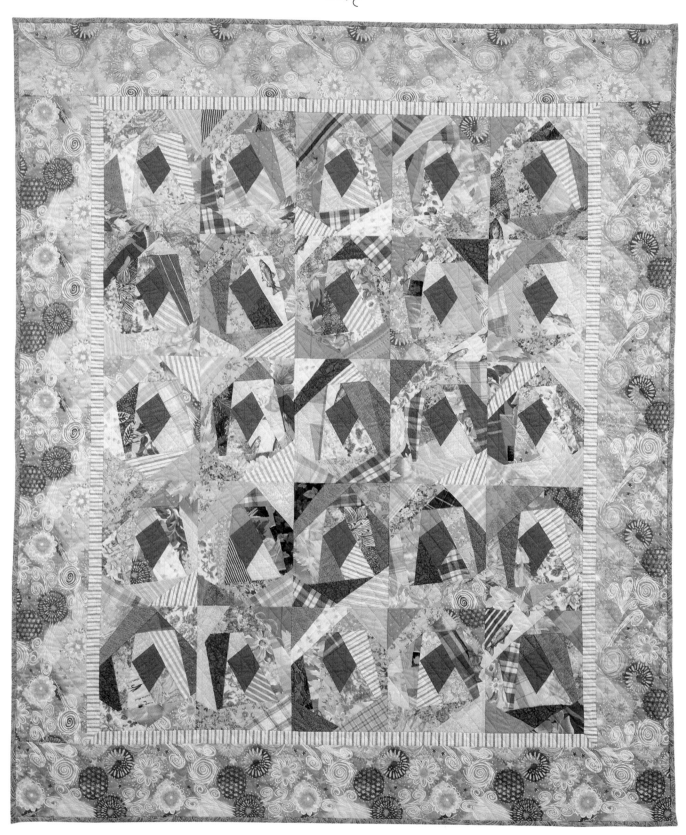

Cabin Fever by Ann Hartig Corkran, 1995, Anchorage, Alaska, 54" x 64". Machine quilted.

By Ann Hartig Corkran

The snow often starts in October and stays through April, resulting in mood swings and a feeling of claustrophobia in our Alaskan quilters.

We brighten our spirits by surrounding ourselves with the colors and fabrics we enjoy. Create your own indoor flower garden using denims, flannels, and cottons to get over that Cabin Fever.

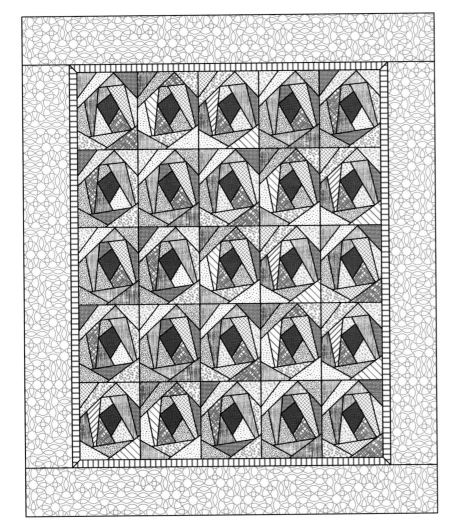

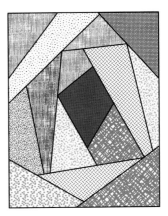

Crazy Patch Log Cabin

Dimensions: 54" x 64"

25 foundation-pieced Crazy Patch Log Cabin blocks, 8" x 10", set 5 across and 5 down; 1"-wide inner border and 6¼"-wide outer border

Materials: 44"-wide fabric

1¾ yds. total assorted scraps of light prints for blocks

¼ yd. medium mauve for block centers

1¾ yds. total assorted scraps of medium prints, including denims and flannels, for blocks

1 yd. total assorted scraps of medium darks for blocks

⅓ yd. light print for inner border

1¼ yds. medium print for outer border

3⅓ yds. backing

½ yd. fabric for 254" of binding

3⅓ yds. 22"-wide Pellon® Stitch-n-Tear® for foundation piecing

Batting

Size 90/14 machine needle (perforates paper and works well with denim)

Cutting

◇ *From the assorted light, medium, and dark prints for blocks, cut:*
6"-wide strips

◇ *From the light print for inner border, cut:*
5 strips, each 1½" x 42"

◇ *From the medium print for outer border, cut:*
6 strips, each 6½" x 42"

◇ *From the Stitch-n-Tear, cut:*
25 rectangles, each 9" x 11"

Directions

Foundation piecing is a quick and easy technique that results in perfectly pieced blocks. A design is drawn on a foundation, then over-size pieces of fabric are placed on the unmarked side of the foundation and seams are sewn from the marked side. It is important to keep in mind that the marked side of the foundation represents the wrong side of the block, and the fabric side is the reverse image of the marked side.

Fabric pieces are added in numerical order. After the seam allowances are trimmed,

the piece is flipped open and pressed. The foundation is removed when the piecing is complete. (Because it is easy to tear from the stitching, Ann likes to use Stitch-n-Tear as a foundation.)

The Cabin Fever block has many different shapes and angles. A simple trick to cutting approximate-size pieces is to hold the fabric with the wrong side toward you while looking at the marked side of the foundation. Cut the fabric large enough to match the needed shape plus extra for seam allowances. When you place the piece, right side up, on the unmarked side of the foundation, it will be the correct shape.

—— Note ——

Set the stitch length to 18 to 20 stitches per inch. The short stitch length perforates the paper and makes removal of the Stitch-n-Tear easier.

—————————

Use block design on pages 92–93.

1. Center each Stitch-n-Tear rectangle over the block design and trace all lines and numbers with a pencil. There will be a ½"-wide margin around the drawn design.

2. Cut the mauve fabric for Piece 1 the approximate size, including at least ¼" for seam allowances on all sides. Position Piece 1 with the wrong side against the *unmarked* side of the foundation rectangle. Make sure the fabric extends at least ¼" beyond the Piece 1 lines on all sides. Hold the foundation and fabric up to a light source to help position the pieces.

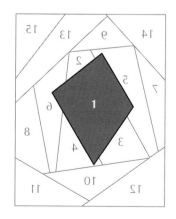

3. Cut the fabric for Piece 2 the approximate size, including at least ¼" for seam allowances on all sides. Place Piece 2 on top of Piece 1, right sides together. Place all the fabrics randomly except for the mauve centers.

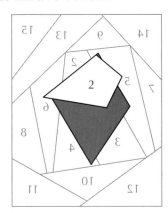

4. With the marked foundation on top, sew on the seam line between Pieces 1 and 2. Sew a few stitches beyond the beginning and end of the line. Trim any excess seam allowance to ¼". Flip Piece 2 open and press

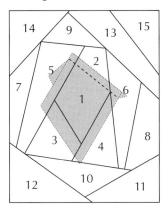

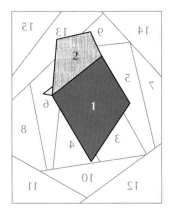

5. Continue adding pieces in numerical order, always keeping the marked foundation on top as you sew, until the

block is complete. Be sure the pieces at the outer edges of the block extend at least ¼" beyond the outer lines of the rectangle. Press the block.

6. Trim the blocks to 8½" x 10½" using a rotary cutter and ruler.

7. Gently remove the Stitch-n-Tear.

8. Set the blocks together in 5 rows of 5 blocks each. Press the seams in opposite directions from row to row. Join the rows.

9. Add the 1½"-wide light inner border, seaming strips as necessary. See "Straight-Cut Corners" on pages 78–79. Repeat with the 6½"-wide medium outer-border strips. The quilt on page 26 was made with mitered borders so that the inner-border stripes would meet in the corners. This isn't necessary with an allover print.

10. Layer the quilt top with batting and backing; quilt or tie. See the quilting suggestion below.

Quilting Suggestion

11. Bind the edges.
12. Label your quilt.

Taking Time to Smell the Flowers

Taking Time to Smell the Flowers, *designed by Dee Morrow; pieced and hand quilted by Clara Limberg, 1995, Anchorage, Alaska, 22" x 25". (Collection of Clara Limberg.)*

Designed by Dee Morrow

Pieced and hand quilted by Clara Limberg

This rough and rugged land is home to rough and rugged individuals. These are people who learn to get by with less, people who live long hours in darkness and snow. Is it any wonder that the beauty and strength of Mother Nature is appreciated here? Spring brings time to smell the flowers.

Dimensions: 23½" x 26⅞"

15" x 18⅜" pieced center; 4¼"-wide border.

Materials: 44"-wide fabric

⅛ yd. each of 6 different background prints
Scraps of dark brown for ears, tail, and legs
⅛ yd. medium brown print for moose body
⅛ yd. light tan print for antlers
⅛ yd. yellow solid for flowers
½ yd. for border
1 yd. for backing
¼ yd. for 98" of binding
½ yd. 4-ply brown wool yarn (optional)
Perle cotton or fabric markers for facial and
  hoof details
2 small, black buttons for eyes (optional)
3 buttons, ⅜" to ½" wide, for flower centers
  (optional)
6 buttons, ⅞" wide, for border (optional)
Batting
Template plastic

Directions

Use the templates on pages 94–101. Make plastic templates of Templates A–F and 1–10. Refer to "Precision Piecing" on page 72.

1. Place Templates A–F right side down on the wrong side of the background fabrics. Using a pencil or marker, outline the template and transfer any markings. Cut ¼" away from the drawn line. Sew the pieces together in alphabetical order. Clip curves where necessary; match the hash marks, and ease to fit. Press the background flat.

2. From the dark brown fabric, cut two 4" squares. Place the 2 squares together, right sides facing. On the wrong side of 1 square, trace 2 ears (Template 10). Sew on the drawn line, leaving the bottom of the ear open. Cut

around each ear, leaving a small seam allowance.

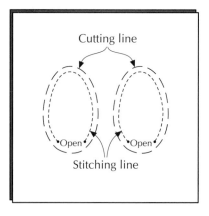

3. Turn the ears inside out. Place the seams of each ear together so the seam is in the middle of the front and back of the ear.

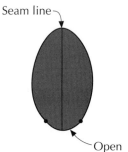

4. Cut appliqué pieces for the moose.

◇ *From the dark brown, cut:*
  1 each of Templates 1, 2, and 5
◇ *From the medium brown, cut:*
  1 each of Templates, 3, 4, 6, 6a, and 9
◇ *From the light tan, cut:*
  1 each of Templates 7 and 8

5. Matching the notches, sew Pieces 6 and 6a together. Treat the resulting piece as a single unit.

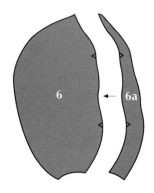

6. Baste the open end of the ears to the head so the raw edges are beneath the turned edges of the head. Pin the pieces in place following the quilt plan on page 31. Appliqué the pieces in numerical order. See "Needle-Turn Appliqué" on page 73.

7. Cut 3 strips from the border fabric, each 4½ " x 42". Add the borders first to the top and bottom edges of the quilt top, then to the sides. See "Straight-Cut Corners" on pages 78–79.

8. Use dark brown embroidery thread or a fabric marker to add the details on the face and hooves. See "Embroidery Stitches" on page 75. Cut short pieces of yarn (about 1" long), untwist the yarns slightly, and glue the yarn between the ears.

9. Layer the quilt top with batting and backing; quilt or tie. See the quilting suggestion below. Use the quilting template on page 94 for the antlers in the border.

10. Bind the edges.

Quilting Suggestion

11. To make 2 small flowers, tear a 1"-wide strip from the width of the yellow fabric. Cut the strip into two 18"-long segments. Snip one side of the fabric as shown, at ¼" to ½" intervals, leaving ¼" on the opposing side uncut. Using 2 strands of quilting thread, gather the uncut side with a long running stitch.

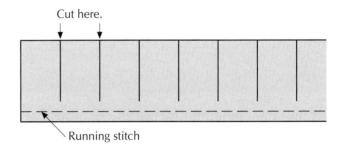

Cut here.

Running stitch

After the strip is tightly gathered, backstitch through the gathered edges to form the flower. Attach the flowers to the quilt with a few stitches in the middle of the flower. To make a large flower, repeat the process with a 1¼"-wide strip. Make as many flowers as you desire.

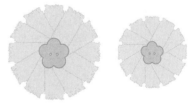

12. Sew a button to the center of each flower and on the border at the midpoint of each quilted antler. Sew on small black buttons for moose eyes.

13. Label your quilt.

Quilter's Totem

Quilter's Totem by Dee Morrow, 1995, Anchorage, Alaska, 24½" x 27½". Hand quilted and tied with buttons.

By Dee Morrow

Alaskan Native folk tales and designs inspired "Quilter's Totem." There is a strong tradition of transformation in Alaskan stories. Men become animals or inanimate objects such as trees or stones. Animals also transform, and the moon has become a man or maiden more than once. Assigning a spirit to a sewing machine follows the tradition. Many times I have felt myself become one with my machine. In keeping with this idea, I designed this quilt to include traditional Alaskan design elements, traditional colors, and buttons reminiscent of button blankets.

Color Key

☐ White

☐ Blue

☐ Red

■ Black

Dimensions: 25" x 28"

16½" x 19½" reverse appliquéd center;
4¼"-wide border

Materials: 44"-wide fabric

½ yd. blue for background
1½ yds. black for top, borders, and 124" of
  binding
⅛ yd. red for accents
⅛ yd. white or off-white for accents
¼ yd. paper-backed fusible web
1 yd. for backing
Assorted buttons
Stars and long bugle beads (optional)
Fine-line, permanent-ink, black fabric-
  marking pen
White or light marking pencil
White DMC perle cotton #5
Batting

Directions

Use the templates on pages 102–105.
**Templates marked with an R are *reverse*
appliquéd.** See "Needle-Turn Appliqué" and
"Reverse Appliqué" on pages 73–74.

--- Tip ---

Match the thread to the background
for reverse appliqué; match the thread
to the appliqué piece for needle-turn
appliqué.

- - - - - - - - -

1. Cut one 17" x 20" rectangle each from
   the blue fabric and the black fabric.
2. Trace Templates 1–20 onto template
   plastic. Carefully cut out the templates.
   Referring
   to the
   quilt plan
   on page
   35, place
   Templates
   1R–7R in
   position
   on the
   right side

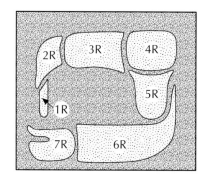

of the blue rectangle. Using a pencil or
marker, outline the templates on the
blue background.
3. Place the black rectangle right side up
   on your work surface. Place the marked
   blue rectangle right side up on top of the
   black rectangle. Baste around the interi-
   ors and exteriors of the 7 design elements.
   Reverse-appliqué the 7 elements.
4. Remove the basting stitches. Carefully
   trim the excess black fabric from the
   back, ¼" beyond the stitching line of
   each design element.

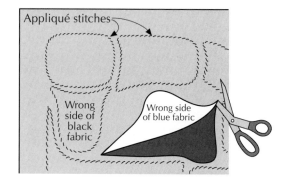

5. Trace Templates 8–10 onto the right
   side of the remaining blue fabric. Cut
   out the shapes, adding a ¼"-wide seam
   allowance. Position the pieces as shown
   below; baste and needle-turn appliqué
   in place.

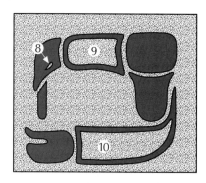

--- Note ---

Add a ⅛"-wide seam allowance to
Piece 8. The piece is small, and the
narrower seam allowance will make
the edges easier to needle turn.

- - - - - - - - -

6. Trace Templates 11–16 onto the right side of the red fabric. Cut out the shapes, adding a ¼"-wide seam allowance. Position the pieces as shown below; baste and needle-turn appliqué. Remove the basting and trim the fabric from the back.

7. Trace Template 17R onto Piece 9, and Template 18R onto Piece 10. Baste inside the drawn shapes and reverse appliqué.

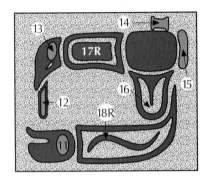

8. To make the face, trace Template 19 onto the paper side of fusible web, including the facial features. Iron the fusible web to the wrong side of the white fabric, following the manufacturer's directions. Using a light table or window to help you see the features, trace the features onto the right side of the fabric. Cut out the crosshatched areas. Use the permanent-ink pen to draw the other lines.

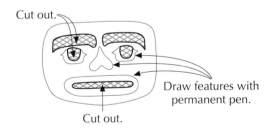

Cut out.

Draw features with permanent pen.

Cut out.

9. Trace Template 20 onto the paper side of the fusible web. Iron onto the wrong side of the red fabric. Cut out Pieces 19 and 20 and peel off the paper backing. Place Piece 19 wrong side down in the middle of Piece 4R. Insert Piece 20 wrong side down under the upper lip of Piece 19. Iron in place. Use a button-

hole stitch on the raw edges. See "Embroidery Stitches" on page 75.

10. From the black fabric, cut 3 strips, each 4½" x 42". Add the borders, following directions for "Straight-Cut Corners" on pages 78–79.

11. Trace 2 of Template 21 onto the right side of the red fabric. Cut out the spools, adding a ¼"-wide seam allowance all around, and appliqué 1 in the upper right corner of the border and 1 in the lower left corner of the border.

12. Layer the quilt top with batting and backing.

13. Lay perle cotton on the quilt top in a meandering fashion, across the top of the machine and in the border. Refer to the photo on page 34 and the quilt plan on page 35. Use white thread to couch the perle cotton every ½". Bring the thread up from underneath, across the perle cotton, and directly back down. Bring the thread up in the same place you brought it up the first time. Go across the perle cotton and take a second stitch down, taking the needle through the batting and bringing it up ½" away. Small stitches will be visible on the front and back of the quilt.

Couching

14. Embellish with beads and buttons. The buttons will anchor the layers. Stay ½" from the outer edge of the quilt to allow for binding.

15. Bind the edges.

16. Label your quilt.

Spirit Houses

Spirit Houses *by Dee Morrow, 1995, Anchorage, Alaska, 25" x 29". Hand quilted.*

By Dee Morrow

Spirit houses are bright, colorful, house-shaped forms found over the graves of departed Alaskan Natives. The belief is that the spirits reside on earth for a period after death and need shelter from the elements.

This quilt depicts a cemetery at the height of summer with flowers in bloom. The houses are shown in two perspectives, along with a Russian Orthodox cross and a picket fence.

Dimensions: 25" x 29"

Spirit House I, 7" x 6"; Spirit House II, 4" x 6"; Picket Fence, 2½" x 4"; no borders

Materials: 44"-wide fabric

¾ yd. grass or flower print
¼ yd. blue print for sky
⅛ yd. black print for cross
¼ yd. white solid for picket fence
⅛ yd. each of 10 to 15 fabrics for spirit houses*
1 yd. for backing
½ yd. for 130" of binding (or use leftover sky and grass fabrics)
Batting
Template plastic

*Or an assortment of scraps.

Cutting

Use the templates on pages 106–107. Refer to "Precision Piecing" on page 72. Reverse templates marked with an r.

◇ *From the grass or flower print, cut:*
7 each of Templates 3, 4, and 5
10 each of Templates 7 and 9
5 each of Templates 11 and 12
6 of Template 14
1 each of Templates 15 and 20
2 each of Templates 16 and 18
3 of Template 21
10 each of Template 23 and 23r

◇ *From the blue print, cut:*
3 each of Templates 3, 4, and 5
1 each of Templates 11 and 12

◇ *From the black print, cut:*
1 each of Templates 16, 17, 18, 19, 21, and 22

◇ *From the white solid, cut:*
10 of Template 24

Spirit House I

◇ *From the assorted ⅛-yard pieces, cut:*
10 each of Templates 1, 2, 6, and 8

---NOTE---

The roofs can be made from a single fabric or pieced using 3 different fabrics. The quilt on page 38 has 4 pieced roofs. Decide which you would like to make for each house. To make a single-fabric roof, use Template 1. To make a 3-piece roof, use Templates 1A, 1B, and 1C.

Spirit House II

◇ *From the assorted ⅛-yard pieces, cut:*
6 each of Templates 10 and 13

Directions

1. Before beginning to piece, lay each block on a piece of batting, flannel, or freezer paper so you can see how the colors interact. Follow the piecing diagrams to piece each block.
2. Piece 10 of Spirit House I.

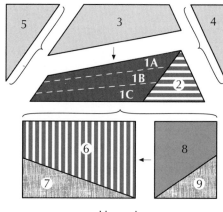

House I
Make 10.

3. Piece 6 of Spirit House II.

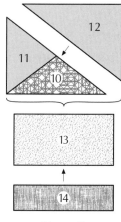

House II
Make 6.

4. Piece 10 Picket Fence units.

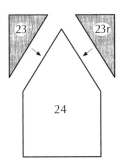

Picket Fence
Make 10.

5. Assemble the 3 sections of the cross. Do not join the sections to each other yet.

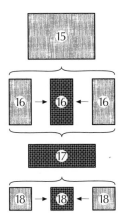

6. Assemble the quilt in horizontal rows as shown. The dotted line indicates where to appliqué the crooked crossbar (Piece 22). See "Needle-Turn Appliqué" on page 73.

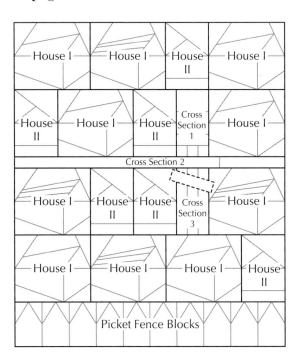

7. Layer the quilt top with batting and backing. Outline quilt the spirit houses and pickets, and stipple the grass and sky.
8. Bind the edges of the quilt with fabrics left over from the quilt top.
9. Label your quilt.

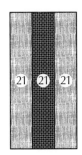

Kuspuk Kate and Parka Pete
"Fly-In Dinner"

Kuspuk Kate and Parka Pete "Fly-In Dinner" by Jean Campbell, 1995, Anchorage, Alaska, 15¾" x 15¾". Machine quilted.

By Jean Campbell ©1995

Jean borrowed from the traditions of Alaskan Natives to create Kuspuk Kate and Parka Pete. This quilt is just one of her fifteen patterns showing Kate and Pete enjoying their Alaskan way of life. These Eskimo children of the Far North are one with their environment. Their teacher is Mother Nature—they live off the land and it is their playground.

Dimensions: 16" x 16"

9½" x 9½" pieced and appliquéd center;
3¼"-wide border

Materials: 44"-wide fabric

⅛ yd. blue print for sky
⅛ yd. blue print for water
⅛ yd. tan print for ground
¾ yd. for border, backing, and binding
⅛ yd. for Mountain 3
Assorted scraps for:
     Mountain 1
     Mountain 2
     Kuspuk (little girl) outfit
     Parka (little boy) outfit
     Trim on sleeves and faces
     Boots, mittens
     Eagle body and wings (black)
     Fish
     Eagle tail and head (white)
Batting
½ yd. paper-backed fusible web
Embroidery floss to match fabrics
Metallic thread

Cutting

❯ *From the blue print for the sky, cut:*
1 rectangle, 4¼" x 10"
❯ *From the blue print for the water, cut:*
1 rectangle, 4⅜" x 10"
❯ *From the tan print, cut:*
1 rectangle, 2⅜" x 10"
❯ *From the fabric for the border, cut:*
2 strips, each 3½" x 10", for side borders
2 strips, each 3½" x 16", for top and bottom
   borders
3 strips, each 2½" x 44", for binding
1 square, 20" x 20", for backing

Directions

Use the templates on page 89.

1. Trace all templates and markings onto the paper side of the fusible web. Cut out the pieces ⅛" to ¼" beyond the drawn lines.
2. Following the manufacturers directions, iron the pieces onto the wrong side of the appropriate fabrics.
3. Carefully cut out each piece and remove the paper backing.
4. Position mountain Pieces 1, 2, and 3 on the sky fabric in numerical order so 1 is underneath 2, and both are underneath 3. Align the bottom of Piece 3 with the lower edge of the sky fabric. Press in place, keeping the iron on the fabrics a few seconds longer than you normally would because of the bulk.

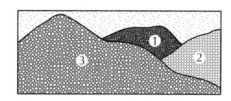

5. Using a ¼"-wide seam allowance, stitch the ground rectangle to the water rectangle, and the sky and mountains to the top of the water. Press all seams toward the bottom.
6. Referring to the diagram at right, place the pieces for Parka Pete and Kuspuk Kate on the background in numerical order. Repeat with the eagle and fish. When you are pleased with the arrangement, press in place.
7. Buttonhole stitch each raw edge. Use metallic thread on the ruffs, cuffs, and tops of the mountains. Use 1 strand of embroidery floss on each of the other raw edges, matching the thread to the fabric. If some pieces are too small for the buttonhole stitch, use a straight stitch to keep them in place. Using metallic thread, chain-stitch around

the edge of the sleeves, across the necks, and on Kuspuk Kate's skirt. See "Embroidery Stitches" on page 75.

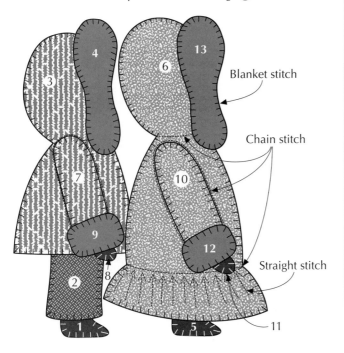

8. Using gold embroidery floss, add a colonial knot for the eagle's eye; embroider the beak and talons using a satin stitch.
9. Using black embroidery floss, make a straight stitch above the eye as shown. This is the hood over the eye.

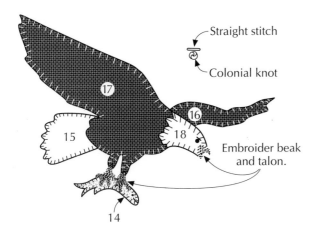

10. Layer the quilt top with batting and backing; quilt or tie. See the quilting suggestion below.

Quilting Suggestion

11. Bind the edges.
12. Label your quilt.

Creative Options: Use the Kuspuk Kate and Parka Pete figures for the front of a pillow, tote bag, or sweatshirt.

Puffins

Puffins by Ramona Chinn, 1987, Anchorage, Alaska, 42" x 42". Hand quilted.

By Ramona Chinn ©1987

The northern puffin, with its chubby shape, orange beak, and web feet, is fun to watch on the steep rocks above the rough ocean waves. These colorful birds are busy and love to be together, as we quilters do. The puffins in this quilt are all individuals, reflecting the personalities of Ramona's quilting friends.

In the quilt on the opposite page, the puffins are appliquéd to a pieced background of black squares and 60° diamonds, which results in irregular edges. The following directions were simplified for easier construction, and therefore will not exactly match the quilt in the color photograph. Only squares are used in the directions for the pieced background, and the edges of the quilt will be straight.

Be creative. Try piecing the background using other patchwork shapes, such as diamonds and strips, or select landscape fabrics in colors to simulate the sky, the water, and a rookery.

Dimensions: 42" x 42"

Materials: 44"-wide fabric

1¾ yds. total of assorted black solids for background (or color combination of your choice)

1⅛ yds. total assorted white-on-black background prints for bodies (minimum 10" x 13")

⅝ yd. total assorted black-on-white background prints for fronts (minimum 6" x 9")

⅛ yd. white solid for faces

Scraps of large black-and-white dot for eyes

Scraps of assorted medium orange prints for beaks and feet (minimum 5" x 5")

Scraps of assorted dark orange prints for yo-yos (minimum 3" x 3")

1½ yds. for backing

¾ yd. black-and-white print for 186" of binding

Batting

2 large sheets of template plastic

Cutting

Use the templates on pages 108–109. Make plastic templates of Templates 1–7. Refer to "Needle-Turn Appliqué" on page 73. Reverse templates marked with an *r*.

◇ *From the assorted black solids, cut a total of:*
49 squares, each 6½" x 6½"

◇ *From the white-on-black background prints, cut a total of:*
8 of Template 1, and 1 of Template 1r; transfer the dots from the pattern onto the fabric pieces using a chalk pencil. These dots include placement of feet, eye, face, and beak.

◇ *From the black-on-white background prints, cut a total of:*
8 of Template 2, and 1 of Template 2r

◇ *From the white solid, cut:*
8 of Template 4, and 1 of Template 4r

◇ *From the black-and-white dot for eyes, refer to step 2 on opposite page and cut a total of:*
8 of Template 3, and 1 of Template 3r

◇ *From the medium orange prints, cut a total of:*
8 each of Templates 5, 6, and 7, and 1 each of Templates 5r, 6r, and 7r

◇ *From the dark orange prints, cut a total of:*
8 of Template 8, and 1 of Template 8r

Directions

Pieced Background

Arrange the assorted black squares in 7 rows of 7 squares each. Sew the squares together in horizontal rows. Press the seams in opposite directions from row to row. Join the rows.

Puffins

See "Making Prairie Points" below.

1. Before beginning, decide whether to add Prairie Points, lace, or ruffles in the seam of Piece 2 (stomach). Embellish each Piece 2 as desired. Appliqué Piece 1 (body) over the edges of the stomach.

━━Making Prairie Points━━

Make Prairie Points by folding 1½" squares in half, then in half again. Place Prairie Points next to each other around the front of the puffin. If you find it difficult to appliqué through all the layers, baste the Prairie Points in place first, then appliqué. Be sure to cover the stitches securing the Prairie Points.

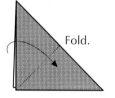
Fold.

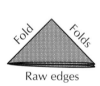
Fold Folds
Raw edges

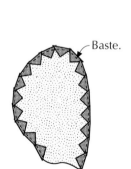
Baste.

2. Pin Piece 3 (eye) in place, matching the dots. Appliqué only the left side of the eye. Leave the right side and the top and bottom edges free.

Appliqué left side only.

---NOTE---

Ramona cut the pieces for the eye so half of a white dot is on the left side.

─ ─ ─ ─ ─ ─ ─ ─ ─

3. Pin Piece 4 (face) in place, matching the dots. Appliqué the face in place, leaving the top edge free.

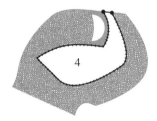

4. Pin Piece 5 (beak) in place, matching the dots. Appliqué only the left side of the beak. Trim the body fabric behind the beak.

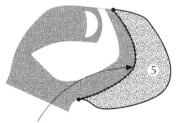

Appliqué left side only.

5. Turn under the seam allowance on Pieces 6 and 7 (feet) and pin in place, matching the dots. Appliqué the body over the top edges of the feet.

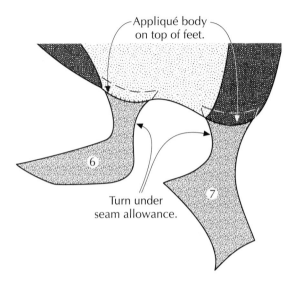

Appliqué body on top of feet.

Turn under seam allowance.

6. Press the puffins.
7. Arrange each puffin on the pieced background. Baste the puffins in place, then appliqué.
8. Make 9 yo-yos, following the directions on page 74. Appliqué in place as indicated by the **X** on the pattern (page 108).
9. Layer the quilt top with batting and backing.
10. Quilt in-the-ditch around each puffin piece and outline-quilt each body. Quilt the background with wavy, irregularly placed horizontal lines to simulate a landscape or air movement.
11. Bind the edges. Use bias strips of fabric if you cut wavy edges on your quilt.
12. Label your quilt.

Creative Options: Use one or two puffins for the front of a pillow, a tote bag, or a sweatshirt. Reduce the pattern to make a child-size version.

Snow Storm

Snow Storm *by Carol Zamarello Johnson, 1995, Anchorage, Alaska, 36" x 36". Machine quilted by Kathy Mosher.*

By Carol Zamarello Johnson

Snow was definitely on our minds, yards, driveways, roads, and roofs in 1994. A record of more than 125″ was set in Anchorage! Supposedly no two snowflakes are alike, so we made each one different in our quilt.

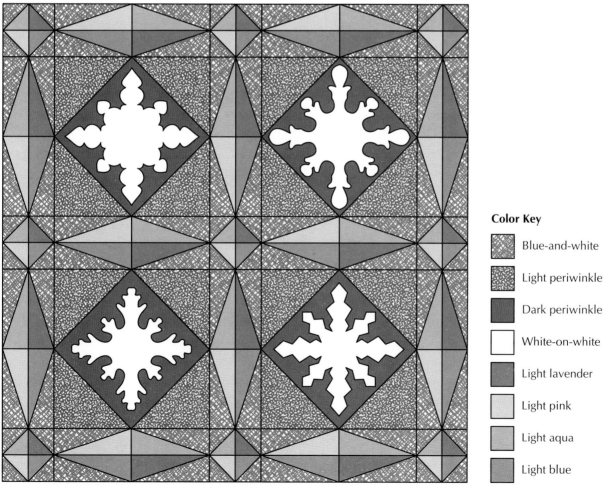

Color Key

- Blue-and-white
- Light periwinkle
- Dark periwinkle
- White-on-white
- Light lavender
- Light pink
- Light aqua
- Light blue

Dimensions: 36" x 36"

4 Square within a Square blocks with appliquéd snowflakes, 12". Set-in 4"-wide pieced sashing and border.

Materials: 44" wide fabric

¾ yd. blue-and-white print
½ yd. light periwinkle print
⅜ yd. dark periwinkle solid
⅜ yd. white-on-white print
⅜ yd. each of light aqua, light blue, lavender, and light pink solids
⅓ yd. paper-backed fusible web
1⅛ yds. for backing
⅜ yd. for 154" of binding
1 ball purple perle cotton or embroidery floss
Embroidery needle
Batting

Cutting

Use the templates on page 110. Reverse templates marked with an *r*.

◇ *From the blue-and-white print, cut:*
  18 squares, each 2⅞" x 2⅞"; cut the squares once diagonally to yield 36 half-square triangles
  24 of Template 1
  24 of Template 1r
◇ *From the light periwinkle print, cut:*
  8 squares, each 6⅞" x 6⅞"; cut the squares once diagonally to yield 16 half-square triangles
◇ *From the dark periwinkle solid, cut:*
  4 squares, each 10" x 10"
◇ *From the white-on-white print, cut:*
  4 squares, each 8½" x 8½"
◇ *From each of the light aqua and light blue solids, cut:*
  5 squares, each 2⅞" x 2⅞"; cut the squares once diagonally to yield 10 half-square triangles
  12 of Template 1
◇ *From each of the lavender and pink solids, cut:*
  5 squares, each 2⅞" x 2⅞"; cut the squares once diagonally to yield 10 half-square triangles
  12 of Template 1r

◇ *From the paper-backed fusible web, cut:*
  4 squares, each 8½" x 8½"

Directions

1. Fold a square of paper-backed fusible web in half, paper side out, then fold in half again to make a square.

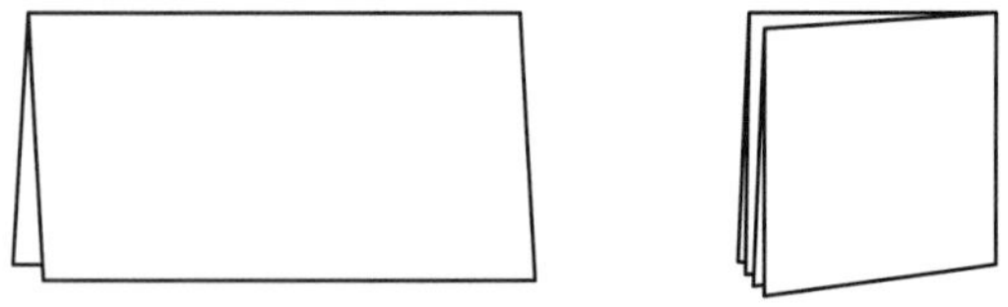

2. Fold the square on the diagonal. Using the patterns on page 110 or designs of your own, lightly outline a snowflake design with a pencil on the paper-backed fusible web. Match the fold lines on the template to the folded edges of the paper. Keeping the paper folded, cut out the snowflake on the line. Make 4 different snowflakes.

Folds

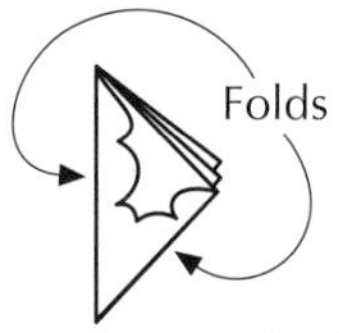

3. Unfold the paper and place the snowflake, web side down, on the wrong side of an 8½" white-on-white square. Following the manufacturer's directions, press the snowflake in place. Cut out the fabric snowflake. Remove the paper.

4. Fold a 10" dark periwinkle square in half, then in half again to find the center. Finger-press the center. Unfold the square, and center the white-on-white snowflake on the right side of the square. Following the manufacturer's directions, press the snowflake onto the square.

5. Buttonhole stitch around the edges of each snowflake. See "Embroidery Stitches" on page 75.

6. Trim the snowflake squares to 9" x 9".

7. Sew 2 light periwinkle half-square triangles to opposite sides of a snowflake

square. Add 2 more half-square tri-angles to the remaining sides to complete Unit A.

Unit A
Make 4.

8. Sew a blue-and-white Piece 1 to each solid color Piece 1 to make a rectangle. Sew a blue-and-white Piece 1r to a solid color Piece 1r. Arrange the rectangles with 1 each of the lavender, pink, aqua, and blue solids in the middle.

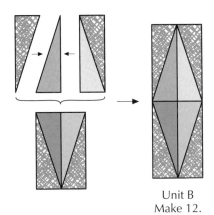

Unit B
Make 12.

9. Sew a blue-and-white half-square triangle to each solid color half-square triangle to make a square. Arrange the squares, with 1 each of the lavender, pink, aqua, and blue solids in the middle.

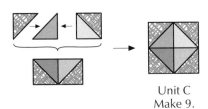

Unit C
Make 9.

10. Join 3 C units and 2 B units to make a row. Make 3 rows.

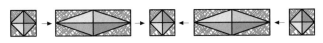

Make 3 rows.

11. Join 3 B units and 2 A units to make a row. Make 2.

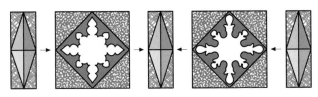

Make 2 rows.

12. Join the rows as shown in the quilt plan on page 51.
13. Layer the quilt top with batting and backing. See the quilting suggestion below. Use a contrasting thread for the veins in the snowflakes.

Quilting Suggestion

14. Bind the edges.
15. Label your quilt.

Borealis Star

Borealis Star by Carol Zamarello Johnson, 1995, Anchorage, Alaska, 48" x 48". Machine quilted by Kathy Mosher.

By Carol Zamarello Johnson

People come from all over the world to see and study the aurora borealis. Colors dance across the sky when this phenomena occurs. Careful placement of beads and light, medium, and dark values captures the aurora's elusive quality.

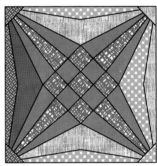

Nine Patch Star

Dimensions: 48" x 48"

9 Nine Patch Stars, 12"; set 3 across and 3 down, 6"-wide border. Colors are arranged to emphasize star shape and light direction.

Materials: 44"-wide fabric

The emphasis in this quilt is on value, not color. Choose an assortment of fabrics for each value, from light to dark (1–9), in whatever color you desire. We chose blue, purple, and aquamarine to depict the midnight sky and the colors of the aurora borealis.

Yardage	Color Number
¼ yd. total	1
⅜ yd. total	2
⅝ yd. total	3
⅝ yd. total	4
⅝ yd. total	5
¾ yd. total	6
⅝ yd. total	7
⅜ yd. total	8
¼ yd. total	9

1 yd. dark print for border
2¼ yds. for pieced backing
½ yd. for 202" of binding
Batting
Bugle beads

Cutting

Use templates on page 111. *Pay attention to the grain line on the templates*. Refer to "Precision Piecing" on page 72. Reverse templates marked with an *r*.

◇ *From the assorted Color 1 fabrics, cut:*
  8 Template E
  2 Template F
◇ *From the assorted Color 2 fabrics, cut:*
  8 Template D
  2 Template F

◇ *From the assorted Color 3 fabrics, cut:*
  4 Template B
  4 Template Br
  4 Template D
  6 Template F
  12 Template E
◇ *From the assorted Color 4 fabrics, cut:*
  12 Template D
  4 Template C
  4 Template E
  6 Template F
◇ *From the assorted Color 5 fabrics, cut:*
  28 Template A
  23 Template B
  23 Template Br
◇ *From the assorted Color 6 fabrics, cut:*
  43 Template A
  5 Template B
  5 Template Br
  24 Template C
  4 Template D
◇ *From the assorted Color 7 fabrics, cut:*
  4 Template E
  5 Template F
  7 Template D
  3 Template C
  2 Template B and 2 Br
  10 Template A
◇ *From the assorted Color 8 fabrics, cut:*
  2 Template B and 2 Br
  7 Template E
  8 Template F
  1 Template C
◇ *From the assorted Color 9 fabrics, cut:*
  1 Template E
  7 Template F
  2 Template C
◇ *From the dark fabric for the border, cut:*
  5 strips, each 6½" x 42"

Directions

----Tip----

Number the upper right-hand corner of each block for ease of placement and construction.

----

1. Following the color placement chart, lay out the pieces for each block so you can see how the colors interact. Precision-piece the templates as follows, pressing after each section is joined:
   a. Join 9 A's to make a nine-patch center.
   b. Sew B to C to Br (make 4 units).
   c. Sew the B/C/Br units to each side of the center nine patch.
   d. Sew D to E (make 4 units).
   e. Set in D/E units.
   f. Add triangle F to each corner.
2. Referring to the color placement chart, sew the blocks in 3 rows of 3 blocks each. Join the rows.
3. Add the 6½"-wide border strips, seaming strips as necessary. See "Straight-Cut Corners" on pages 78–79.

4. Layer the quilt top with batting and backing. Quilt or tie. Because of the number of seams in this quilt, it was machine quilted in straight lines radiating from the center of the light star into the borders
5. Attach beads to give the quilt a "twinkling star" quality.
6. Bind the edges.
7. Label your quilt.

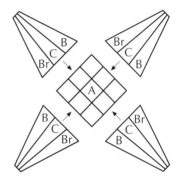

Color Placement Chart

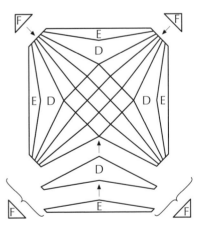

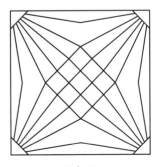

Make 9.

Chugach Summer

By Jeanie Smith

We have a wonderful, ever-changing view of the Chugach Mountains outside our shop window. They are covered with snow for about seven months of the year, and for the other five months they are in a constant state of flux, showing greens, yellows, golds, reds, and browns.

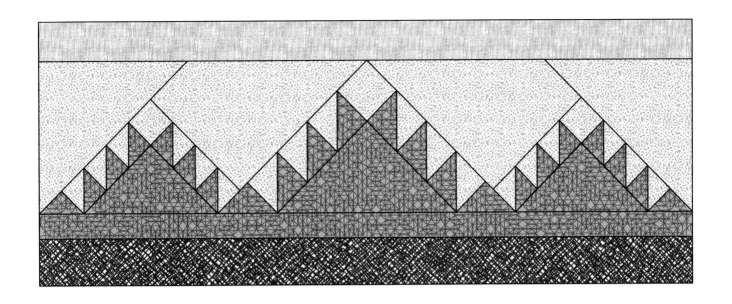

Chugach Summer by Jeanie Smith, 1995, Anchorage, Alaska, 18" x 45". Machine quilted by Jean Campbell.

Dimensions: 18" x 45"

1 Delectable Mountains half-block, 15", and 2 Delectable Mountains half-blocks, 11¼", set in a single row; 3"-wide top border, 1¾"-wide mountain-base strip, and 3½"-wide bottom border.

Materials: 44"-wide fabric

¾ yd. tapestry print
⅝ yd. light blue print
¼ yd. ivory print for top border
¼ yd. green print for bottom border
1½ yds. for backing
⅜ yd. for 148" of binding
Batting

Cutting

◇ *From the tapestry print, cut:*
   2 strips, 2¼" x 42", for mountain-base strip
   1 strip, 3⅞" x 42"; crosscut the strip into 1 segment, 3⅞" x 13", and 1 square, 3⅞" x 3⅞". Cut the square once diagonally to make 2 half-square triangles.
   1 strip, 3⅛" x 42"; crosscut the strip into 1 segment, 3⅛" x 20", and 1 square, 3⅛" x 3⅛". Cut the square once diagonally to make 2 half-square triangles.
   1 square, 9⅞" x 9⅞"; cut the square once diagonally to make 2 half-square triangles. You will use only 1 of the triangles.
   1 square, 7⅝" x 7⅝"; cut the square once diagonally to make 2 half-square triangles

◇ *From the light blue print, cut:*
   1 strip, 3⅞" x 42". From one end of the strip, cut 1 segment, 3⅞" x 13". From the rest of the strip, cut 1 square, 3½" x 3½", and 2 squares, 2¾" x 2¾".
   1 strip, 3⅛" x 42". From this strip, cut 1 segment, 3⅛" x 20".
   1 square, 11½" x 11½"; cut the square once diagonally to make 2 half-square triangles
   2 rectangles, each 9½" x 13⅝"

◇ *From the ivory print, cut:*
   2 strips, each 3¼" x 42"

◇ *From the green print, cut:*
   2 strips, each 3¾" x 42"

Directions

1. See "Quick Half-Square Triangle Units" on pages 71–72. Layer the 3⅞" x 13" tapestry print and light blue strips, right sides together. Cut 3 squares, 3⅞" x 3⅞", from the strip pair. Cut the squares once diagonally and chain-piece the resulting triangle pairs to make 6 half-square triangle units.

2. Join the half-square triangle units, the 3⅞" tapestry print half-square triangles, the 9⅞" tapestry print half-square triangle, and the 3½" light blue square to make the large mountain as shown.

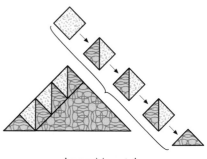

Large Mountain
Make 1.

3. Layer the 3⅛" x 20" tapestry print and light blue strips, right sides together, to make 1 contrasting strip pair. Cut 6 squares, each 3⅛" x 3⅛", from the strip pair. Cut the squares once diagonally and chain-piece the resulting triangle pairs to make 12 half-square triangle units.

4. Join the half-square triangle units, the 3⅛" tapestry print half-square triangles, the 7⅝" tapestry print half-square triangles, and the 2¾" light blue squares to make small mountains A and B as shown. Note that the small mountains have 3⅛" tapestry print triangles on the outside edges only.

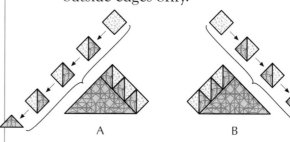

A   B

Small Mountains
Make 1 of each.

5. Trim the corners of the 9½" x 13⅝" light blue rectangles at a 45° angle as shown, to make Pieces A and B.

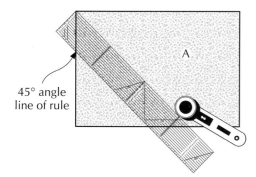

45° angle line of rule

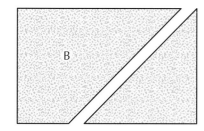

6. Join Pieces A and B to the small mountain blocks as shown.

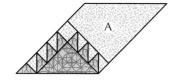

7. Join the mountains and the 11½" light blue half-square triangles.

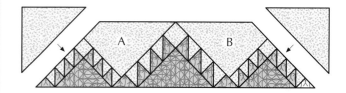

8. Joining strips as necessary for required length, add a 2¼"-wide tapestry print strip to the bottom of the mountains, a 3¾"-wide green print strip below that, and a 3¼"-wide ivory print strip to the top of the mountains.

9. Layer the quilt top with batting and backing. Quilt; see the quilting suggestion below.

10. Bind the edges.

11. Label your quilt.

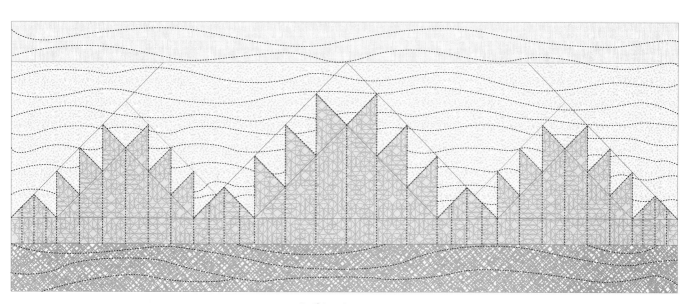

Quilting Suggestion

Crow's Foot

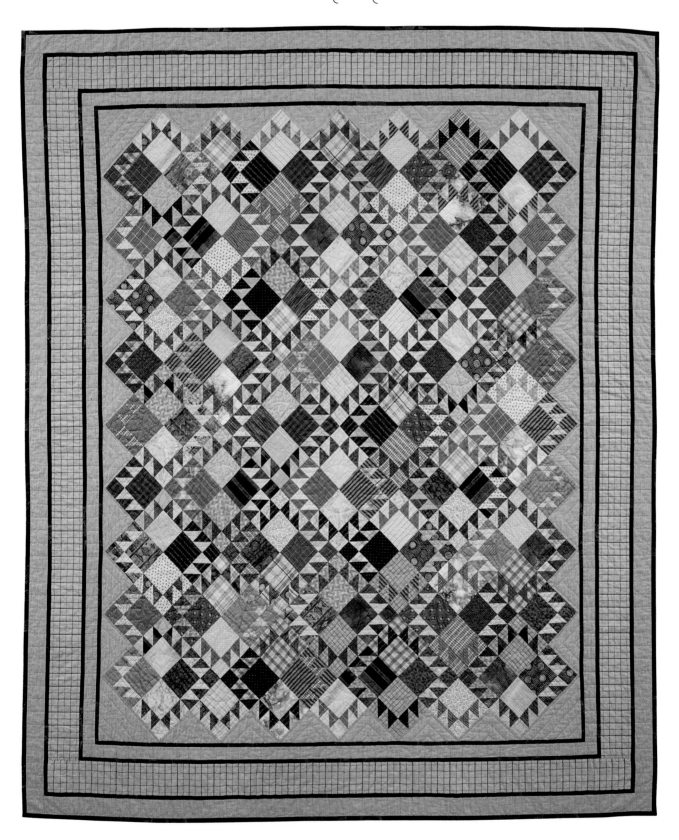

Crow's Foot by Judy Hopkins, 1995, Anchorage, Alaska, 77¼" x 92½". Hand quilted.

By Judy Hopkins

In the Tlingit culture of southeastern Alaska, it is believed that the Raven created the earth. Therefore, it seemed only appropriate to make the Crow's Foot block with forest greens and sky blues, and to float them within the many borders.

Crow's Foot

Dimensions: 78" x 92¾"

32 Crow's Foot blocks, 10½", and 14 quarter-blocks, set on point 4 across and 5 down with ¼" float; 9"-wide border made from ½", 1½", ½", 3¾", ½", and 2¼" strips

Materials: 44"-wide fabric

¼ yd. each of 18 different light prints in blue and green for blocks

¼ yd. each of 18 different dark prints in blue, green, and red-violet for blocks

2 yds. light blue check for setting triangles and borders

⅞ yd. red-violet print for borders

1⅛ yds. light blue windowpane plaid for seamed border

5⅝ yds. for backing (lengthwise seam)

¾ yd. for 360" of binding

Batting

Cutting

◇ *From each of the 18 light prints in blue and green, cut:*

1 strip, 2⅝" x 42", for a total of 18 strips; cut each strip into 8 segments, each 2⅝" x 5¼", for a total of 142 rectangles

4 squares, each 4" x 4", for a total of 70 squares

4 squares, each 2¼" x 2¼", for a total of 70 squares

——Note——

If your fabric is less than 42" wide, cut the eighth rectangle from scraps after cutting the squares.

——————————

◇ *From each of the 18 dark prints in blue, green, and red-violet, cut:*

1 strip, 2⅝" x 42", for a total of 18 strips; cut each strip into 8 segments, each 2⅝" x 5¼", for a total of 142 rectangles

4 squares, each 4" x 4", for a total of 72 squares

4 squares, each 2¼" x 2¼", for a total of 72 squares

◇ *From the light blue check, cut:*

2 strips, each 9⅜" x 42"; cut the strips into a total of 7 squares, each 9⅜" x 9⅜". Cut the squares twice diagonally to make 28

quarter-square triangles for side-setting triangles

2 squares, each 9" x 9"; cut the squares once diagonally to make 4 half-square triangles for corner-setting triangles

8 strips, each 2" x 42", for second border

9 strips, each 2¾" x 42", for sixth border

◇ *From the red-violet print, cut:*

25 strips, each 1" x 42", for inner, third, and fifth borders

◇ *From the light blue windowpane plaid, cut:*

8 strips, each 4¼" x 42", for fourth border

Directions

1. Sort the light blue and green rectangles and the dark blue, green, and red-violet rectangles into 142 pleasing sets, each containing one light piece and one dark piece. Use as many different fabric combinations as possible.

2. Add one 4" and one 2¼" dark blue, green, or red-violet square to each of 72 of the rectangle sets, matching the dark squares to the dark rectangle in each set.

3. Add one 4" and one 2¼" light blue or green square to each of the remaining 70 rectangle sets, matching the light squares to the light rectangle in each set.

4. Start with the sets that have dark squares. Work with one set at a time. See "Quick Half-Square Triangle Units" on pages 71–72. Layer the dark rectangle and the light rectangle, right sides together, to make a contrasting strip pair. Cut 2 squares from the layered strips, each 2⅝" x 2⅝", for a total of 2 layered squares. Cut the squares once diagonally and chain-stitch the resulting triangle pairs along the long edges to make 4 half-square triangle units.

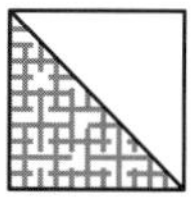

5. Join the half-square triangle units and the matching 4" and 2¼" dark squares to make 1 Unit A as shown. Repeat

steps 4 and 5 with each of the remaining dark-square sets to make a total of 72 A units.

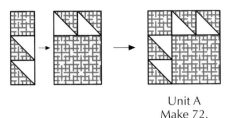

Unit A
Make 72.

6. Working with one light-square set at a time, make half-square triangle units as described in step 4.

7. Join the half-square triangle units and the matching light squares to make 1 Unit B as shown. Repeat steps 6 and 7 with each of the remaining light-square sets to make a total of 70 B units.

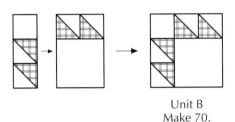

Unit B
Make 70.

8. Using 64 A units and 64 B units, combine units randomly to piece 32 Crow's Foot blocks as shown.

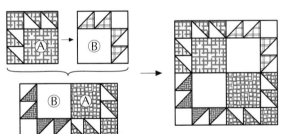

Make 32.

9. Join the 9⅜" light blue check side setting triangles to the remaining Unit A and Unit B pieces to make 8 dark and 6 light pieced setting triangles as shown.

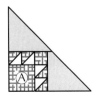
Make 8.

Make 6.

After sewing one triangle, trim the dog ear, then add the second triangle. The setting triangles are cut large to allow for the float.

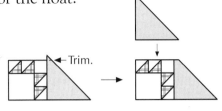

10. Set the blocks and setting triangles together in diagonal rows, referring to the quilt plan on page 63. Place the dark setting triangles along the sides, and the light setting triangles on the top and bottom. Join the rows. Add the corner setting triangles last. Trim the outside edges and square up the corners of the quilt as necessary, leaving ½" of fabric outside the block corners to allow the blocks to float. See "On-Point Sets" on pages 77–78.

11. Attach the border strips to the quilt in the following order, seaming as necessary: 1" red-violet, 2" check, 1" red-violet, 4¼" windowpane plaid, 1" red-violet, 2¾" check. See "Straight-Cut Corners" on pages 78–79.

12. Layer the quilt top with batting and backing; quilt or tie. See the quilting suggestion below.

Quilting Suggestion

13. Bind the edges.

14. Label your quilt.

Tippler's Track

Tippler's Track by George Taylor, 1995, Anchorage, Alaska, 44" x 56". Machine quilted.

By George Taylor

"Eight stars of gold on a field of blue" is the opening line of the Alaska state song, and blue and gold are Alaska's state colors. This scrap quilt, a variation of Drunkard's Path, evokes memories of the intense colors of Alaskan skies.

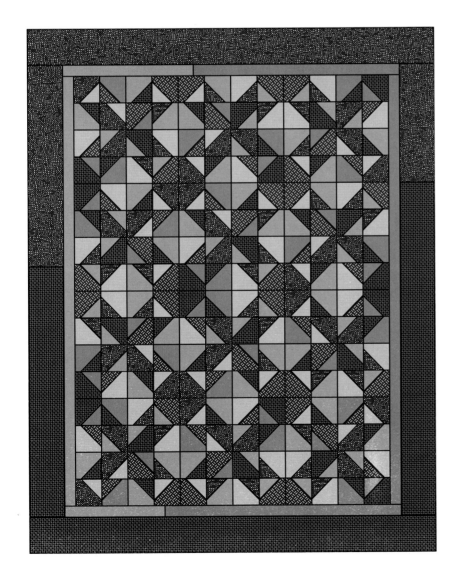

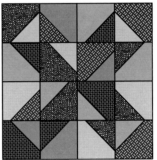

Tippler's Track

Dimensions: 46½" x 58½"

12 blocks, 12", set 3 across and 4 down; 1¼"-wide inner border, 4"-wide outer border

Materials: 44"-wide fabric

¼ yd. each of 5 different bright blue prints for blocks
½ yd. each of 3 more bright blue prints for blocks and outer border
¼ yd. each of 5 different yellow solids ranging from pale yellow to lemon to gold, for blocks
⅓ yd. each of 3 more yellow solids for blocks and inner border
3 yds. for backing (crosswise seam)
½ yd. for 228" of binding
Batting

Cutting

All measurements include ¼"-wide seam allowances.

◇ *From each of the ¼-yd. pieces of blue prints, cut:*

1 strip, 3½" x 42", for a total of 5 strips; cut strips into a total of 60 squares, each 3½" x 3½"
1 strip, 2⅞" x 42", for a total of 5 strips; cut strips into a total of 60 squares, each 2⅞" x 2⅞"

◇ *From each of the ½-yd. pieces of blue prints, cut:*

1 strip, 3½" x 42", for a total of 3 strips; cut strips into a total of 36 squares, each 3½" x 3½"
1 strip, 2⅞" x 42", for a total of 3 strips; cut strips into a total of 36 squares, each 2⅞" x 2⅞"
2 strips, each 4¼" x 42", for the outer border

◇ *From each of the ¼-yd. pieces of yellow solids, cut:*

1 strip, 3½" x 42", for a total of 5 strips; cut strips into a total of 60 squares, each 3½" x 3½"
1 strip, 2⅞" x 42", for a total of 5 strips; cut strips into total of 60 squares, each 2⅞" x 2⅞"

◇ *From each of the ⅓-yd. pieces of assorted yellow solids, cut:*

1 strip, 3½" x 42", for a total of 3 strips; cut strips into a total of 36 squares, each 3½" x 3½"
1 strip, 2⅞" x 42", for a total of 3 strips; cut strips into a total of 36 squares, each 2⅞" x 2⅞"
2 strips, each 1¾" x 42", for the pieced inner border

Directions

1. Draw a diagonal line from corner to corner on the wrong side of each of the 2⅞" yellow squares. Place a yellow square on top of a 3½" blue square, right sides together, as shown. Stitch on the drawn line and trim the corner ¼" from the stitching line. Make 96 blue squares with yellow corners, combining fabrics randomly.

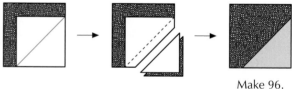

Make 96.

2. Draw a diagonal line from corner to corner on the wrong side of each of the 2⅞" blue squares. Place a blue square on top of a 3½" yellow square, right sides together, as shown. Stitch on the drawn line and trim the corner ¼" from the stitching line. Make 96 yellow squares with blue corners, combining fabrics randomly.

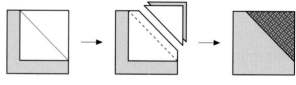

Make 96.

3. Piece 12 Tippler's Track blocks, following the piecing diagram. Press the seams in opposite directions from row to row. Join the rows. Press the seams in one direction.

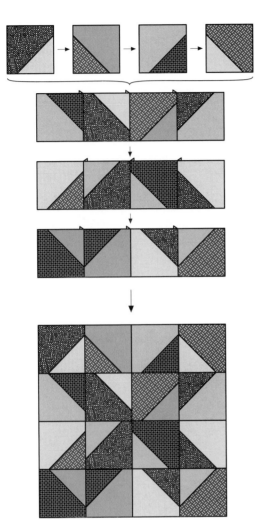

Make 12.

4. Set the blocks together in 4 rows of 3 blocks each, following the quilt plan on page 67. Join the rows.

5. Cut the 1¾"-wide yellow inner-border strips into random lengths and join as needed to make side, top, and bottom borders. Stitch to the quilt top, following directions for "Straight-Cut Corners" on pages 78–79. Repeat with the 4¼"-wide blue outer-border strips.

6. Layer the quilt top with batting and backing; quilt or tie. See the quilting suggestion below.

Quilting Suggestion

7. Bind the edges.
8. Label your quilt.

General Directions

Fabric Preparation

Calicoes & Quilts Unlimited has one of the finest selections of cotton fabrics in Alaska. We love fabrics and carry a multitude of plaids, stripes, batiks, tone-on-tones, solids, hand-dyed fabrics, large and small prints, and flannels.

The method you will use to clean your finished quilt determines how you need to prepare your fabric. If you are going to wash or dry-clean your quilt, rinse your fabric in warm water to test the stability of the dyes. If a fabric bleeds, add ½" cup of white vinegar to the water, then heat-set in the dryer and test again. If you plan to add embellishments and will only be dusting it off, there is no need to prewash.

We used cottons, flannels, and denims for the quilts in this book, reflecting the ruggedness and colors of our great outdoors. If you want to match the look and feel of our quilts, refer to the color photographs before selecting fabrics.

Rotary Cutting

I think the rotary cutter is the greatest thing since sliced bread, and I am not sure I would have continued quilting if I could use only scissors. Despite my love for rotary cutting, templates have their place in this book as well, so make sure you have paper scissors and sharp fabric scissors.

The following is my preferred method for rotary cutting:

1. Fold the fabric in half, selvage to selvage, keeping the fabric smooth. Fold the fabric again so that the first folded edge is even with the selvages. The fabric should measure about 11" wide.
2. Place the second folded edge parallel to the bottom edge of the rotary mat.

Align a horizontal line on the ruler with the bottom fold and a vertical line with the side edge of your mat, and cut off the uneven raw edge of the fabric.

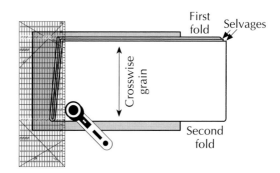

3. To cut strips, align the desired measurement on the ruler with the cut edge of the fabric, then cut along the ruler's edge. Periodically check your strips to make sure they are straight. You might need to repeat step 2.

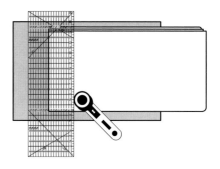

4. To cut squares and rectangles, cut strips in the required widths. Trim the selvages. Align the desired measurement on the ruler with the left edge of the strips and cut a square or rectangle. Continue cutting pieces until you have the required number.

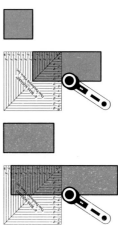

Piecing Methods

This book features two machine-piecing techniques: Template-Free® and Precision. Template-Free piecing includes ¼"-wide seam allowances in the cutting measurements; precision piecing requires templates that do not include ¼"-wide seam allowances. Template-Free does not necessarily mean easy. Make sure you read through the directions before beginning a project.

Template-Free Piecing

In Template-Free piecing, all cutting measurements include ¼"-wide seam allowances. Therefore, it is important that you establish an accurate ¼" sewing guide on your machine before you begin piecing.

---Tip---

I like to use a scant ¼"-wide seam allowance because of the small amount of fabric that is taken up when seams are pressed to one side.

Do not use the edge of the presser foot as a guide until you have verified the distance from the needle to the right-hand edge of the foot. Lay a piece of ¼"-grid paper under the presser foot. Place the needle on the inside of the ¼" line. Does the edge of the presser foot fall at the edge of the graph paper? If it does, you can safely use the foot for piecing. If it doesn't, you may be able to adjust the needle to the right or left. If you can't adjust the needle, make a guide by applying a piece of masking tape on the throat plate along the right edge of the graph paper as shown below.

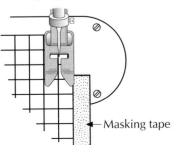

← Masking tape

Check your newly set, scant-¼" guide by sewing together three 1½"-wide strips of fabric. Press the seams and measure across the center of the strip set—it should be 3½" wide. If it is not, adjust your sewing guide and try again.

Stitching Seams

To join pieces of fabric, place them right sides together, aligning the raw edges. Stitch from raw edge to raw edge unless otherwise instructed. It is not necessary to backstitch because all seams will be crossed by another seam. Even the stitching along the outermost edges of your quilt top will be secured when the border or binding is attached.

Quick Half-Square Triangle Units

Half-square triangle units typically consist of two contrasting triangles stitched together along the long edge to form a square.

Every quilter has a favorite method for making these units. Some quilters draw and stitch grids, others cut and seam bias strips and then cut bias squares. The patterns in this book feature an easy layered-strip technique that produces little waste. Yardage and yield calculations are simple and straightforward, so are more likely to be accurate.

To make half-square triangle units, assemble strip pairs by layering contrasting strips or strip segments, right sides together, with the long edges aligned. (When working with several fabrics in each color or value group, use as many different fabric combinations as possible.) If you press the strip pairs after aligning the fabrics, they will stick together, reducing the possibility of slippage during the crosscutting process and making it unnecessary to pin when you sew.

Cut squares from each layered pair of strips following the pattern instructions.

Cut the layered squares once diagonally from corner to corner.

Chain-piece the resulting triangle pairs to make half-square triangle units. The pairs are ready to sew. Cut the units apart and trim the corners before pressing.

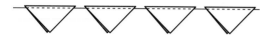

Precision Piecing

This method requires templates that do not include a ¼"-wide seam allowances. Seam allowances are added when the pieces are cut from fabric.

1. Trace the pattern pieces onto template plastic. Transfer any hash marks, grainline arrows, identifying words, numbers, and letters onto the plastic template. Carefully cut out the templates. Verify the templates by laying them on top of the pattern and checking for differences.

2. Place the template face down on the wrong side of the fabric. Using a pencil or marker, outline the template and transfer any markings. The outline is your sewing line. Leave at least ½" between pieces for seam allowances.

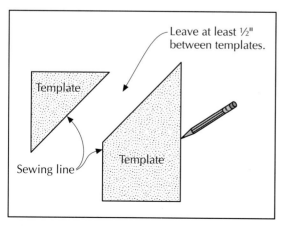

Leave at least ½" between templates.

Template

Template

Sewing line

3. Cut out the pieces, adding a ¼"-wide seam allowance all around. You can eyeball this—the measurement does not need to be precise.

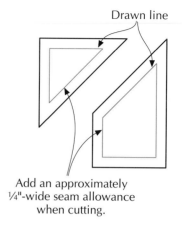

Drawn line

Add an approximately ¼"-wide seam allowance when cutting.

4. Pin the pieces right sides together, aligning the corners and any hash marks. Place pins so that they penetrate the sewing line on both pieces. Sew from the edge across the drawn line to the opposite edge. Check the pieces to be sure the stitches follow the marked sewing lines on both front and back.

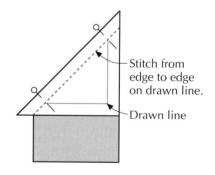

Stitch from edge to edge on drawn line.

Drawn line

Appliqué Techniques

Needle-Turn Appliqué

This appliqué method is easy to master with just a little practice.

1. Trace the pattern pieces onto template plastic. Transfer any hash marks, grain lines, identifying words, numbers, or letters onto the plastic template. Carefully cut out the templates.
2. Place the template face up on the right side of the fabric. Using a pencil or marker, outline the template. The outline is your sewing line. Leave at least ½" between pieces for seam allowances.
3. Cut out the pieces, adding a ³/₁₆"- to ¼"-wide seam allowance all around.
4. Pin the wrong side of the appliqué piece to the right side of the background fabric. Baste in place.
5. Beginning on a straight edge or gentle curve, use the tip of the needle to turn under the seam allowance a thread or two beyond the marked seam line. Turn under about ½" of the seam allowance at a time, holding it between the thumb and first finger of your left hand (reverse if left-handed). Use a blind stitch to secure the edges.

Blind Stitch

This is the most common appliqué stitch.

1. Tie a knot in a single strand of 18"-long thread. Bring the needle up from the wrong side of the background fabric and catch a few threads right at the sewing line of the appliqué piece. Stab your needle into the background fabric at about the same spot you came up. Travel about ⅛" under the background fabric in a clockwise manner and come up into the appliqué piece, catching only a thread or two of the folded edge. Pull

the thread tightly and continue stitching. Turn the seam allowance under as you progress. You may need to make a small clip in the seam allowance on tight curves or sharp angles so the appliqué piece will lie flat.

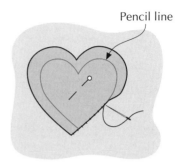

Pencil line

2. To end your stitches, pull the needle through to the wrong side. Take 2 small stitches behind the appliqué piece and knot the end of the thread.

Reverse Appliqué

In reverse appliqué, layered fabrics are carefully cut to reveal the fabric beneath. The raw edges are then appliquéd with a blind stitch.

1. Trace the pattern pieces onto template plastic. Transfer any hash marks, grain lines, identifying words, numbers, or letters onto the plastic templates. Carefully cut out the templates.
2. Place the plastic templates face up on the right side of the background fabric. Using a pencil or marker, outline the template. This is the sewing line.
3. Place the wrong side of the background fabric on top of the right side of the appliqué fabric. Baste about ½" along both sides of the sewing line.

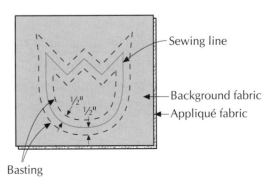

Sewing line

Background fabric
Appliqué fabric

½"
½"

Basting

4. Carefully make a small cut in the background fabric (top layer only), ⅜" inside the sewing line. Cut along the innermost basting line, gradually decreasing the seam allowance to ¼". Clip inside and outside curves to the seam line as necessary.

Clip when necessary.

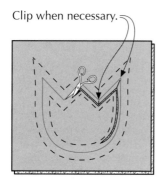

5. Turn under the seam allowance so the drawn line does not show. Use a blind stitch to appliqué the folded edges. Remove the basting stitches.

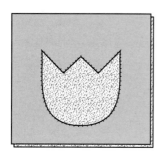

Fusible-Web Appliqué

Paper-backed fusible web provides a quick and easy way to achieve the look of appliqué without all the work. Appliqués are attached to a background with the fusible web's heat-activated glue rather than with stitches.

1. Use a No. 2 pencil to trace the pattern onto the paper side of the fusible web.
2. Cut out the patterns ⅛" to ¼" beyond the drawn line; you don't need to be precise. Following the manufacturer's directions, press the pieces onto the wrong side of the selected fabric.

3. Carefully cut out each piece on the drawn lines. Small, sharp scissors are very useful.
4. Remove the paper and place the pieces on your background fabric. Tweezers are helpful for placing small pieces in position.
5. Hand or machine embroider the raw edges if your finished piece is to be cleaned or handled at all.

Making Yo-yos

These adorable gathered fabric circles add texture to "Puffins" on page 46.

1. Cut a circle of fabric using the pattern on page 108.
2. Knot a single strand of quilting thread. With the wrong side of the fabric facing you, fold over and baste a ⅛"-wide seam allowance all around.

3. Tighten the stitches, forming a small bag. Flatten the bag into a circle, centering the gathered edge. You can either knot the thread at this time or use it to attach the yo-yo to the puffin.

Embroidery Stitches

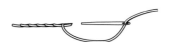

Straight Stitch

Stem Stitch

Colonial Knot

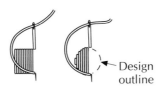

Design outline

Buttonhole Stitch

Satin Stitch

Chain Stitch

Detached Chain or Lazy Daisy Stitch

Finishing Your Quilt

The following text has been used, all or in part, from Down the Rotary Road with Judy Hopkins *with permission from the author.*

This section begins with basic information on squaring up blocks and joining them in either straight or on-point (diagonal) sets, and continues with an in-depth discussion of other finishing techniques: adding borders, marking the quilting lines, preparing backing and batting, layering the quilt, quilting and tying, binding, and adding sleeves and labels. The quilts in this book feature a variety of finishing approaches, and the photos are an excellent source of ideas.

Squaring Up Blocks

Some quiltmakers find it necessary to trim or square up their blocks before they assemble them into a quilt top. If you trim, be sure to leave ¼"-wide seam allowances beyond any points or other important block details that fall at the outside edges of the block.

If your block is distorted and doesn't look square, square it up. To square a block, cut a piece of plastic-coated freezer paper to the proper size (finished block size plus seam allowance), and iron the freezer paper to your ironing-board cover, plastic side down. Align the block edges with the edges of the freezer-paper guide and pin. Gently steam press. Allow the blocks to cool before you unpin and remove them.

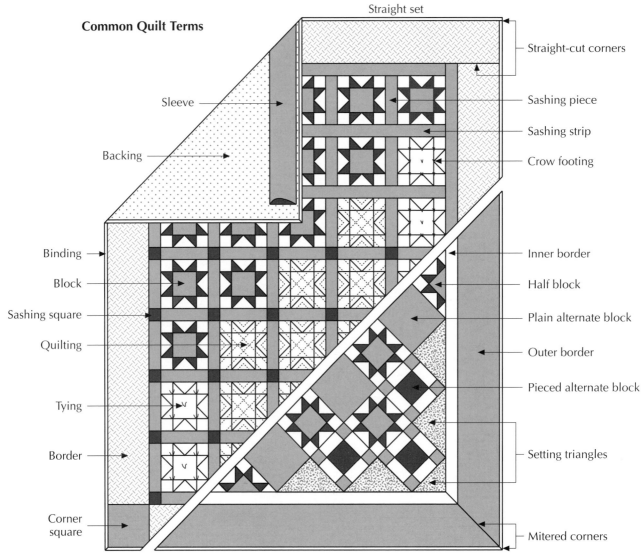

Common Quilt Terms

Straight set

Straight-cut corners

Sashing piece

Sashing strip

Crow footing

Sleeve

Backing

Binding

Block

Sashing square

Quilting

Tying

Border

Corner square

Inner border

Half block

Plain alternate block

Outer border

Pieced alternate block

Setting triangles

Mitered corners

On-point (diagonal) set

Straight Sets

In straight sets, blocks are laid out in rows that are parallel to the edges of the quilt. Constructing a straight-set quilt is simple. When you set blocks side by side, simply stitch them together in rows. Press the seams in opposite directions from row to row, then join the rows to complete the patterned section of the quilt. If you are using alternate blocks, cut or piece them to the same size as the primary blocks (including seam allowances), then lay out the primary and alternate blocks in checkerboard fashion and stitch them together in rows.

On-Point Sets

Quilts laid out with the blocks set on point are constructed in diagonal rows. To avoid confusion, lay out all the blocks and setting pieces in the proper configuration before you start sewing. In an on-point set in which blocks are set side by side without sashing, simply pick up and sew one row at a time, then join the rows.

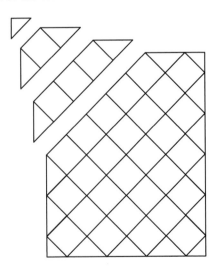

When you use the cut 'em big approach for the setting triangles, the side and corner triangles will be larger than the blocks. Align the square corners of the triangle and the block when you join the side triangles to the blocks, leaving the excess at the "point" end of the setting triangle. Stitch and press the seam, then trim the excess even with the edge of the block.

Attach the corner triangles last, centering the triangles on the blocks so any excess or shortfall is distributed equally on each side.

When sewn, your quilt top will look something like this:

Obviously, you will need to do some trimming and squaring up. At this point, you can make a decision about whether to leave some excess fabric so the blocks will float or to trim the setting triangles so only a ¼"-wide seam allowance remains. Use the outside corners of the blocks to align your cutting guide and trim as desired. Make sure the corners are square.

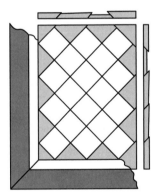

Trimming to leave ¼" seam allowance. Border, when added, will come to the corners of the blocks.

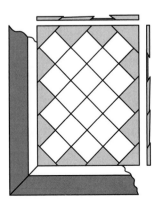

Trimmed to allow blocks to float.

Finishing Your Quilt ◆ **77**

Some of us have difficulty getting on-point quilts to lie flat. You can minimize potential problems by taking a few precautions during the cutting and assembly process. Make sure the individual blocks are absolutely square and are all the same size. Plain or pieced alternate blocks should be perfectly square and exactly the same size as the primary blocks. The 90° corners of the side setting triangles should be truly square. Since these triangles are quick-cut on the bias, sometimes the corners are not square. It's worth taking the time to double-check. When you join blocks to setting triangles, feed them into the sewing machine with the block, which has a straight-grain edge, on top and the bias-edged setting triangle on the bottom.

Borders

Whether to add a border to your quilt is entirely up to you. Some quilts seem to resist borders. If you have tried several border options and none seems to work, perhaps the piece wants to be finished without a border or with a border on only one or two sides. Many quilts will happily accept a "1-2-3" border—an inner border, a middle border, and an outer border in 1:2:3 proportions (1" inner, 2" middle, and 3" outer borders, or 1½" inner, 3" middle, and 4½" outer borders, for example).

Though many of us avoid adding elaborately pieced borders to our quilts because of the additional work involved, some quilts demand them. As an alternative, try a multi-fabric border. Use a different fabric on each edge of the quilt. Use one fabric for the top and right edges, and a different fabric for the bottom and left edges; or join random chunks of several different fabrics until you have pieces long enough to form borders. Quiltmakers who buy fabric in small cuts often resort to multi-fabric borders out of necessity, as they rarely have enough of any one fabric to border an entire quilt!

Because you need extra yardage to cut borders on the lengthwise grain, plain border strips commonly are cut along the crosswise grain and seamed when extra length is needed. Press these seams open for minimum visibility. To ensure a flat, square quilt, cut border strips extra long and trim the strips to the proper length after you know the actual dimensions of the patterned center section of the quilt.

Most of the quilts in this book have seamed borders with straight-cut corners; a few have borders with mitered corners.

Straight-Cut Corners

Mitered Corners

Straight-Cut Corners

To make a border with straight-cut corners, measure the length of the patterned section of the quilt at the center, from raw edge to raw edge. Cut two border strips to that measurement and join them to the sides of the quilt top with a ¼"-wide seam allowance, matching the ends and centers and easing the edges to fit. Measure the width of the quilt at the center from edge to edge, including the border pieces you just added. Cut two border strips to this measurement and join them to the top and bottom of the quilt, matching ends and centers and easing as necessary.

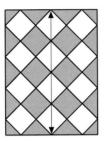
Measure length at center.

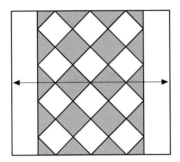
Measure width at center after adding side borders.

--Note--

Do not measure the outer edges of the quilt. Often, edges measure longer than the quilt center due to stretching during construction; the edges might even be different lengths. To keep the finished quilt as straight and square as possible, you must measure the center.

Mitered Corners

To make mitered corners, first estimate the finished outside dimensions of your quilt, including borders. Cut border strips to this length plus at least ½" for seam allowances. It's safer to add 2" to 3" to give yourself leeway. If your quilt will have multiple borders,

sew together the individual strips and treat the resulting unit as a single piece.

Mark the centers of the quilt edges and the centers of the border strips. Stitch the borders to the quilt top with a ¼"-wide seam allowance, matching the centers; the border strip should extend the same distance at each end of the quilt. Start and stop your stitching ¼" from the corners of the quilt; press the seams toward the borders.

Lay the first corner to be mitered on the ironing board, pinning as necessary to keep the quilt from pulling and the corner from slipping. Fold one of the border units under at a 45° angle. Work with the fold until seams or stripes meet properly; pin at the fold, then check to see that the outside corner is square and that there is no extra fullness at the edges. When everything is straight and square, press the fold.

Starting at the outside edge of the quilt, center a piece of 1"-wide masking tape over the mitered fold. Remove pins as you apply the tape.

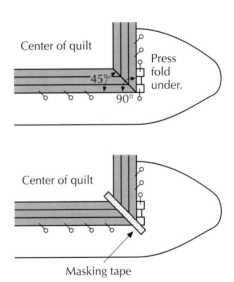

Unpin the quilt from the ironing board and turn it over. Draw a light pencil line on the crease created when you pressed the fold. Fold the center section of the quilt diagonally from the corner, right sides together, and align the long edges of the border strips. Stitch on the pencil line; remove the tape. Trim excess fabric and press the seam open. Repeat these steps for the remaining three corners.

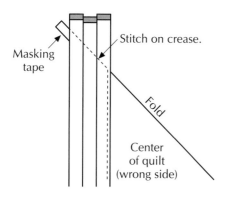

Masking tape

Stitch on crease.

Fold

Center of quilt (wrong side)

Marking Quilting Lines

Marking may not be necessary if you are planning to quilt in-the-ditch or to outline quilt a uniform distance from seam lines. Some quiltmakers do outline quilting by eye, though many others use ¼"-wide masking tape to mark these lines as they stitch. You can use masking or drafting tape to mark any straight-line quilting design. Cut simple shapes from Con-Tact® paper. Apply the tape or adhesive-paper shape when you are ready to quilt and remove promptly after you have quilted along its edge. Adhesives left on the quilt too long can leave a residue that is difficult to remove.

Mark complex quilting designs on the quilt top before layering it with batting and backing. A gridded transparent ruler is useful for measuring and marking straight lines and filler grids. If the quilt fabrics are fairly light, you can place quilting patterns from books or magazines or hand-drawn designs underneath the quilt and trace onto the fabric. Use a light box or put your work against a window if you have difficulty seeing the design.

If you cannot see through the quilt fabric, you will need to draw the design directly onto the quilt top. Use a precut plastic stencil, or make one by drawing or tracing the quilting

design on clear plastic. Cut out the lines with a double-bladed craft knife, leaving bridges every inch or two so the stencil will hold its shape. You can also trace the design onto plain paper (or make a photocopy). Cover the paper with one or two layers of clear Con-Tact paper and cut out the lines. Try putting small pieces of double-stick tape on the back of the stencil to keep it in place as you mark the quilting lines.

When marking quilting lines, work on a hard, smooth surface. Use a hard lead pencil (No. 3 or 4) on light fabrics; for dark fabrics, try a fine-line chalk marker or a silver, nonphoto blue, or white pencil. Ideally, marking lines will remain visible for the duration of the quilting process and will be easy to remove when the quilting is done. Light lines are always easier to remove than heavy ones; test to make sure the markings will wash out after the quilting is completed.

If you are using an allover quilting pattern that does not relate directly to the seams or to a design element of the quilt, you may find it easier to mark the quilting lines on the backing fabric and quilt from the back rather than from the front of the quilt.

Backings

The quilt backing should be at least 6" wider and 6" longer than the quilt top. A length of 44"-wide fabric (42 useable inches after preshrinking) is adequate to back a quilt that is no wider than 36". For a larger quilt, buy extrawide cotton or sew together two or more pieces of fabric. Use a single fabric, seamed as necessary, to make a backing of adequate size, or piece a simple multi-fabric back that complements the front of the quilt. Early quiltmakers often made pieced backings as a matter of necessity; modern quiltmakers see quilt backings as another place to experiment with color and design.

If you opt for a seamed or pieced backing, trim selvages before you stitch, and press seams open.

Calculate the yardage required for single-fabric backings as follows:

For quilts up to 36" wide, any length: length + 6"
For quilts 37" to 78" wide and no longer than 78": width + 6" x 2 (1 crosswise seam)
For quilts 37" to 78" wide and more than 78" long: length + 6" x 2 (1 lengthwise seam)
For quilts more than 78" wide and 79" to 120" long: width + 6" x 3 (2 crosswise seams)

Batting

Batting comes packaged in standard bed sizes; you can also buy it by the yard. Several weights or thicknesses are available. Thick battings are fine for tied quilts and comforters; choose a thinner batting if you intend to quilt by hand or machine.

Thin batting is available in 100% cotton, 100% polyester, and an 80%/20% cotton-polyester blend. Supposedly, the blend combines the best features of the two fibers. All-cotton batting is soft and drapable but requires close quilting and produces quilts that are rather flat. Though many quilters like the antique look, some find cotton batting difficult to needle. Glazed or bonded polyester batting is sturdy and easy to handle, and it washes well. It requires less quilting than cotton and has more loft. Polyester fibers, however, sometimes migrate through fabric, creating tiny white "beards" on the surface of a quilt. The dark gray and black polyester battings now available may ease this problem for quiltmakers who like to work with dark fabrics. Bearding, if it occurs, is less noticeable.

Unroll your batting and let it relax overnight before you layer your quilt. Some battings need to be prewashed, while others should definitely not be prewashed. Be sure to check the manufacturer's instructions.

Layering the Quilt

Once you have marked your quilt top, pieced and pressed your backing, and let your batting relax, you are ready to layer the quilt. Spread the backing, wrong side up, on a flat, clean surface; anchor it with pins or masking tape. Spread the batting over the backing, smoothing out any wrinkles. Then center the quilt top on the backing, right side up. Be careful not to stretch or distort any of the layers as you work. Starting in the middle, pin-baste the three layers together, gently smoothing any fullness to the sides and corners.

Baste the three layers together with a long needle and light-colored thread; start in the center and work diagonally to each corner, making a large **X**. Continue basting, laying in a grid of horizontal and vertical lines 6" to 8" apart. Finish by basting around the outside edges.

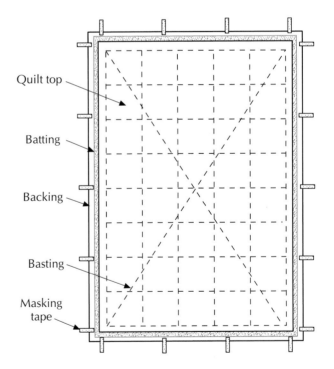

Quilt top

Batting

Backing

Basting

Masking tape

Quilting

The purpose of quilting or tying is to keep the three layers together and to prevent the batting from lumping or shifting. Quilts typically are tied with knots either on the front or the back, or they are machine or hand quilted. Quiet exploration is taking place in this facet of quiltmaking. While several old methods for tying and quilting are being revived, some quiltmakers are stretching tradition by "tying" with eyelets or decorative studs, or quilting with unusual materials, such as ribbon, wire, and even cassette tape.

Machine Quilting

Machine quilting is suitable for all types of quilts, from simple baby and bed quilts that will be washed frequently to sophisticated pieces for the wall. With machine quilting, you can quickly complete quilts that might otherwise languish on the shelf.

Unless you plan to stitch in-the-ditch or do free-motion quilting, mark the quilting lines before you layer the quilt. Consider using a simple allover grid or a continuous-line quilting design. Basting for machine quilting is usually done with safety pins. If you have a large work surface to support the quilt and an even-feed foot for your sewing machine, you should have no problem with shifting layers or untidy pleats, tucks, and bubbles on the back side.

At the beginning of a line of quilting, pull the bobbin thread to the top. Hold the threads to prevent them from tangling and take a few tiny stitches in place. This locks the threads. At the end of a line of quilting, take another few tiny stitches in place to lock the threads. Carefully clip the thread tails.

Try machine quilting with threads of unusual types and weights, or experiment with the decorative stitch or twin-needle capabilities of your sewing machine. Twin-needle quilting produces an interesting, corded effect.

Traditional Hand Quilting

To quilt by hand, you need short, sturdy needles (called "Betweens"), quilting thread, and a thimble to fit the middle finger of your sewing hand. Most quilters also use a frame or hoop to support their work. Quilting needles run from size 3 to 12. The higher the number, the smaller the needle. Use the smallest needle you can comfortably handle; the smaller the needle, the smaller your stitches will be.

Thread your needle with a single strand of quilting thread about 18" long. Make a small knot and insert the needle in the top layer about 1" from the place you want to start stitching. Pull the needle out at the point where quilting will begin and gently pull the thread until the knot pops through the fabric and into the batting.

Begin your quilting line with a backstitch and continue with a small, even running stitch. Place your left hand underneath the quilt so you can feel the needle point with the tip of a finger when you take a stitch.

Push the needle through all the layers with the thimbled middle finger of your top hand, using the dimples in the side or end of the thimble (whichever is more comfortable) to support the eye end of the needle. When you feel the tip of the needle with the middle or index finger of the underneath hand, simultaneously rock the needle eye toward the quilt surface, depress the fabric in front of the needle with the thumb of the top hand, and push the needle tip up with the underneath finger.

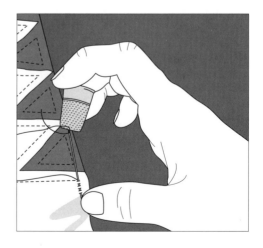

When the needle tip comes through to the top of the quilt, relax the top-hand thumb and the underneath finger, rock the needle eye up so it is almost perpendicular to the quilt, and push the needle through the layers to start the next stitch. Repeat the process until you have three or four stitches on the needle, then pull the needle all the way through, taking up any slack in the thread, and start again.

To end a line of quilting, make a small knot close to the last stitch; then backstitch, running the thread a needle's length through the batting. Gently pull the thread until the knot pops into the batting. Clip the thread at the quilt's surface. Remove basting stitches as you quilt, leaving only those that go around the outside edges of the quilt.

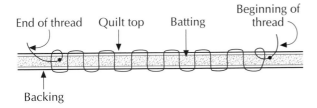

Utility Quilting

Utility quilting is faster than traditional hand quilting but homier than machine quilting. You use big needles and heavy threads (like perle cotton, crochet thread, or several strands of embroidery floss) and take big stitches, anywhere from 1/8" to 1/4" in length. The method is well worth considering for casual, scrappy quilts and for pieces you might otherwise plan to machine quilt. Quilts finished with this technique are sturdy, and the added surface texture is very pleasing.

You can do utility quilting freehand, without marking the quilt top, or mark quilting lines as usual. Use the shortest, finest, sharpest needle you can get the thread through; try several different kinds to find the needle that works best for you. I like working with #8 perle cotton and a #6 Between needle. Keep your stitches as straight and even as possible.

Crow Footing

Crow footing is done with a long needle and thick thread, such as a single or double strand of perle cotton or crochet thread. Isolated fly stitches are worked in a grid across the surface of the quilt, leaving a small diagonal stitch on the back of the quilt. There are no visible knots or dangling threads. Stitches can be spaced as far apart as the length of your needle will allow.

Put your work in a hoop or frame. Use a long, sharp-pointed needle—try cotton darners, millinery needles, or soft-sculpture needles. Make a small knot in the thread and insert the needle in the top layer of the quilt about 1" from A. Pull the needle out at A and gently pull the thread until the knot pops through the fabric and into the batting. Hold the thread down with your thumb and insert the needle at B as shown; go through all three layers and bring the needle out at C. Insert the needle at D and travel through the top layer only to start the next stitch at A.

Work in rows from the top to the bottom or from the right to the left of the quilt, spacing the stitches 2" to 3" apart. To end stitching, bring the needle out at C and make a small knot about 1/8" from the surface of the quilt. Make a backstitch at D, running the thread through the batting an inch or so; pop the knot into the batting and clip the thread at the surface of the quilt.

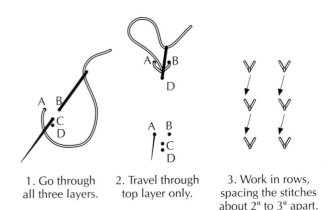

1. Go through all three layers.

2. Travel through top layer only.

3. Work in rows, spacing the stitches about 2" to 3" apart.

Crow Footing

You can do these stitches at random, rather than on a uniform grid. Early quiltmakers often worked with the quilt stretched full size on a large floor frame, working from both ends and rolling in the edges of the quilt as the rows of tacking were completed, thus eliminating the need for basting. You can tie or tack small quilts without basting if you spread the layers smoothly over a table or other large, flat work surface.

Tying

Tying is quick method for finishing a quilt that will get a lot of wear and tear. Baby quilts and all-purpose quilts are great candidates for tying.

Use perle cotton, yarn, or six strands of embroidery floss and a long-eye needle to make threading easier. Take a ¼" stitch at each spot you want a tie. Do not cut the threads between the ties. The thread should be loose between the stitches to allow enough room to tie the ends into a knot. I like to make a tie every 4".

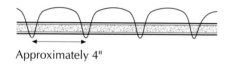

Approximately 4"

When you finish all the ties, cut the thread between the stitches and tie a square knot (right over left, then left over right). Trim the ends to about 1". You can space the ties evenly in horizontal and vertical lines across the quilt surface or in a random pattern; but be sure to keep them within 4" of each other.

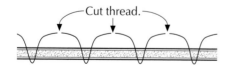

Cut thread.

——Note———

For tying, it isn't necessary to baste the layers together.

Binding

When the tying or quilting is complete, prepare for binding by removing any remaining basting threads, except for the stitches around the outside edge of the quilt. Trim the batting and backing even with the edge of the quilt top. Use a rotary cutter and cutting guide to get accurate, straight edges; make sure the corners are square.

Make enough binding to go around the perimeter of the quilt, plus about 18". The general instructions below are based on ⅜"-wide (finished), double-fold binding, which is made from strips cut 2½" wide and stitched to the outside edges of the quilt with a ⅜"-wide seam allowance. Cutting dimensions and seam widths for bindings in other sizes are given in the chart on page 86.

Straight-grain binding is fine for most applications. Simply cut strips from the lengthwise or crosswise grain of the fabric; one crosswise strip will yield about 40" of binding. For ⅜"-wide (finished) binding, cut the strips 2½" wide. Trim the ends of the strips at a 45° angle and seam the ends to make a long, continuous strip; press the seams open.

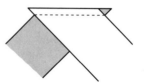
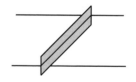

Cut strip ends at a 45° angle and seam.

Press seam allowances open.

Fold the strip in half lengthwise, wrong sides together, and press.

Use bias binding if your quilt edge has curves or if you expect the quilt to get heavy use; binding cut on the bias wears longer. Some quilters cut bias strips from a flat piece of fabric, joining the strips after cutting.

To make flat-cut bias binding, lay out a length of fabric. (Fabric requirements are given below.) Make a bias cut starting at one corner of the fabric; use the 45° marking on a long cutting ruler as a guide. Then cut bias strips, measuring from the edges of the initial bias cut. For 3/8"-wide (finished) binding, cut the strips 2½" wide. Seam the ends to make a long, continuous strip; press the seams open. Fold the strip in half lengthwise, wrong sides together, and press.

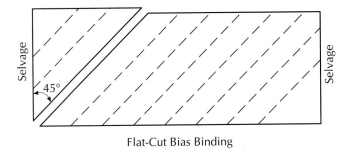

Flat-Cut Bias Binding

◇ *For 3/8"-wide (finished) binding made from 2½"-wide strips:*

¼ yard fabric yields about 115" of binding
3/8 yard fabric yields about 180" of binding
½ yard fabric yields about 255" of binding
5/8 yard fabric yields about 320" of binding
¾ yard fabric yields about 400" of binding
7/8 yard fabric yields about 465" of binding

Two methods for applying the binding to the quilt are described below. The first method produces a binding with mitered corners, and the binding is applied in a continuous strip around the edges of the quilt. In the second method, measured lengths of binding are applied separately to each edge of the quilt. In both cases, the instructions given are based on 3/8"-wide finished binding. You will need to use a different seam width if your finished binding is narrower or wider than 3/8".

Bindings with Mitered Corners

For a binding with mitered corners, start near the center of one side of the quilt. Place the binding on the front of the quilt, lining up the raw edges of the binding with the raw edges of the quilt. Using an even-feed foot, sew the binding to the quilt with a 3/8"-wide seam allowance. Leave the first 8" to 10" of the binding loose so you can join or overlap the

beginning and ending of the binding strip later. Be careful not to stretch the quilt or the binding as you sew. When you reach the corner, stop the stitching 3/8" from the edge of the quilt and backstitch; clip threads.

Turn the quilt to prepare for sewing along the next edge. Fold the binding up and away from the quilt; then fold it again to bring it along the edge of the quilt. There will be an angled fold at the corner. The straight fold should be even with the top edge of the quilt.

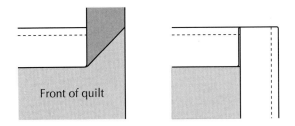

Front of quilt

Stitch from the straight fold in the binding to the next corner, pinning as necessary to keep the binding lined up with the raw edge of the quilt. When you reach the next corner, stop the stitching 3/8" from the edge of the quilt and backstitch; clip threads. Fold the binding as you did at the last corner and continue around the edge of the quilt. Stop and backstitch about 12" from the starting point. Overlap the end of the remaining unattached binding and the tail you left when you started and adjust them to fit the quilt exactly. Join with a diagonal seam; trim the excess. Stitch this newly joined section to the quilt.

Fold the binding to the back, over the raw edges of the quilt; the folded edge of the binding should just cover the machine stitching line. Blindstitch the binding in place, making sure your stitches do not go through to the front of the quilt. At the corners, fold the binding to form miters on the front and back of the quilt; stitch down the folds in the miters.

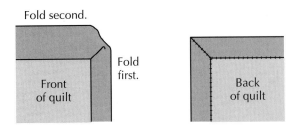

Fold second.

Front of quilt

Fold first.

Back of quilt

Bindings with Measured Strips

Use this binding method if the outside edges of your quilt need to be eased to the binding so their finished measurements conform to the quilt's center measurements. Straight-grain binding strips work best for this type of binding.

Bind the long edges of the quilt first. Measure the length of the quilt at the center, raw edge to raw edge.

——Note——

Do not measure the outer edges of the quilt. Often the edges measure longer than the quilt center due to stretching during construction; the edges might even be different lengths.

————————

From your long strip of binding, cut two pieces of binding to the lengthwise center measurement. Working from the right side of the quilt, pin the binding strips to the long edges of the quilt, matching the ends and centers and easing the edges to fit as necessary. Use an even-feed foot and sew the binding to the quilt with a ⅜"-wide seam allowance. Fold the binding to the back, over the raw edges of the quilt; the folded edge of the binding should just cover the machine-stitching line. Blindstitch the binding in place, making sure your stitches do not go through to the front of the quilt.

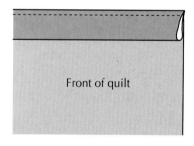

Front of quilt

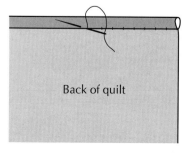

Back of quilt

Measure the width of the quilt at the center, outside edge to outside edge. From the remainder of your long binding strip, cut two pieces to that measurement plus 1". Pin these measured binding strips to the short edges of the quilt, matching the centers and leaving ½" of the binding extending at each end; ease the edges to fit as necessary. Sew the binding to the quilt with a ⅜"-wide seam allowance.

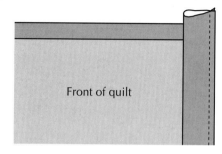

Front of quilt

To finish, fold the extended portion of the binding strips down over the bound edges; then bring the binding to the back and blindstitch in place as before.

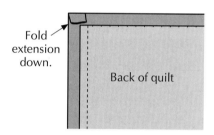

Fold extension down.

Back of quilt

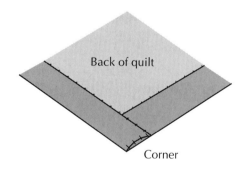

Back of quilt

Corner

————————

Strip and seam widths for double-fold bindings in various finished sizes are as follows:

Binding	Strip Width	Seam
¼"	1¾"	¼"
⅜"	2½"	⅜"
½"	3¼"	½"
⅝"	4"	⅝"
¾"	4¾"	¾"

————————

Sleeves and Labels

Quilts that will be displayed on walls should have a sleeve tacked on the back near the top edge to hold a hanging rod. I put sleeves on all my quilts, even those intended for beds, so they can be safely hung if they are suddenly requested for an exhibit or if their owners decide to use them for decoration rather than as bedding.

Sleeves should be a generous width. Use a piece of fabric 6" to 8" wide and 1" to 2" shorter than the finished width of the quilt at the top edge. Hem the ends, then fold the fabric strip in half lengthwise, wrong sides together. Seam the long, raw edges together with a ¼"-wide seam allowance. Fold the tube so the seam is centered on one side; press the seam open.

Hem ends, then seam raw edges, right side out.

Center seam and press open.

Place the tube on the back side of the quilt, just under the top binding, with the seamed side against the quilt. Hand sew the top edge of the sleeve to the quilt, taking care not to catch the front of the quilt as you stitch.

Tack down top edge of sleeve.

Push the tube up so the top edge covers about half of the binding (providing a little "give" so the hanging rod does not put strain on the quilt itself), and sew the bottom edge of the sleeve in place as shown.

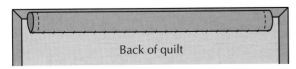

Push tube up and tack down bottom edge.

Slide a curtain rod, a wooden dowel, or a piece of lath through the sleeve. The seamed side of the sleeve will keep the rod from coming into direct contact with the quilt. Suspend the rod on brackets. Or, attach screw eyes or drill holes at each end of the rod and slip the holes or eyes over small nails.

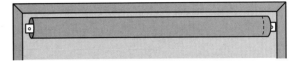

Insert hanging rod in sleeve.

Be sure to sign and date your work! At the very least, embroider your name and the year you completed the quilt on the front or back of the quilt. Quilt historians and future owners of your quilts will want to know more than just the "who" and "when." Consider tacking a handwritten or typed label to the back of the quilt that includes the name of the quilt, your name, your city and state, the date, whom you made the quilt for and why, and any other interesting or important information about the quilt.

Press a piece of plastic-coated freezer paper to the wrong side of the label fabric to stabilize it while you write or type. For a handwritten label, use a permanent marking pen; use a multistrike ribbon for typewritten labels. Always test to be absolutely sure the ink is permanent.

——Note——

Hand- or typewritten labels that safely pass the washing-machine test sometimes run and bleed when they are dry-cleaned.

————————

Products Available

Kuspuk Kate and Parka Pete patterns and Calicoes & Quilts Unlimited sweatshirts and T-shirts depicting the quilts can be obtained from:

Calicoes & Quilts Unlimited
11900 Industry Way
Anchorage, AK 99515

Additional patterns with Kuspuk Kate and Parka Pete:

Skiing
Puffins
Glacier
Dog Sled
Watching the Northern Lights
Berry Picking
Look at the Moose
Practicing for the Blanket Toss
Fishing
Airplane
Favorite Fishing Hole
Kayaking
On Our Way to Church
Bringing Home the Tree

Templates

Kuspuk Kate and Parka Pete
Appliqué Templates

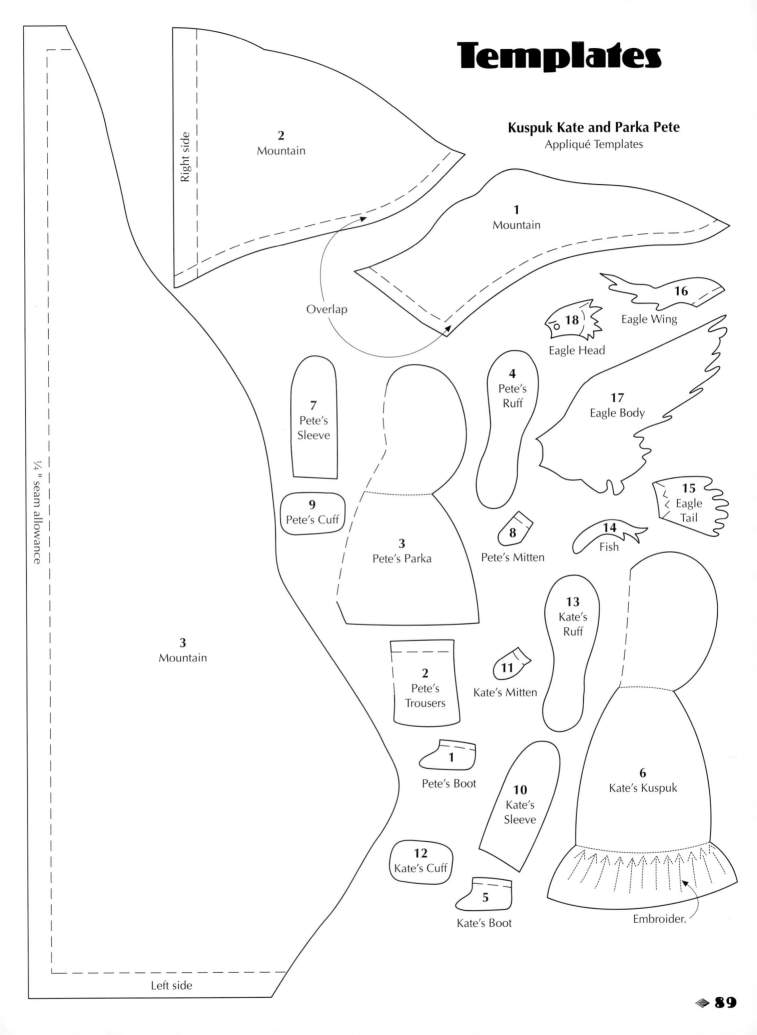

Right side

2
Mountain

¼" seam allowance

3
Mountain

Left side

Overlap

1
Mountain

16
Eagle Wing

18
Eagle Head

17
Eagle Body

15
Eagle Tail

7
Pete's Sleeve

9
Pete's Cuff

3
Pete's Parka

4
Pete's Ruff

8
Pete's Mitten

14
Fish

13
Kate's Ruff

2
Pete's Trousers

11
Kate's Mitten

1
Pete's Boot

10
Kate's Sleeve

12
Kate's Cuff

5
Kate's Boot

6
Kate's Kuspuk

Embroider.

Blowing in the Wind
Appliqué Templates
Flowers

Pleat lines

1

2

3

4

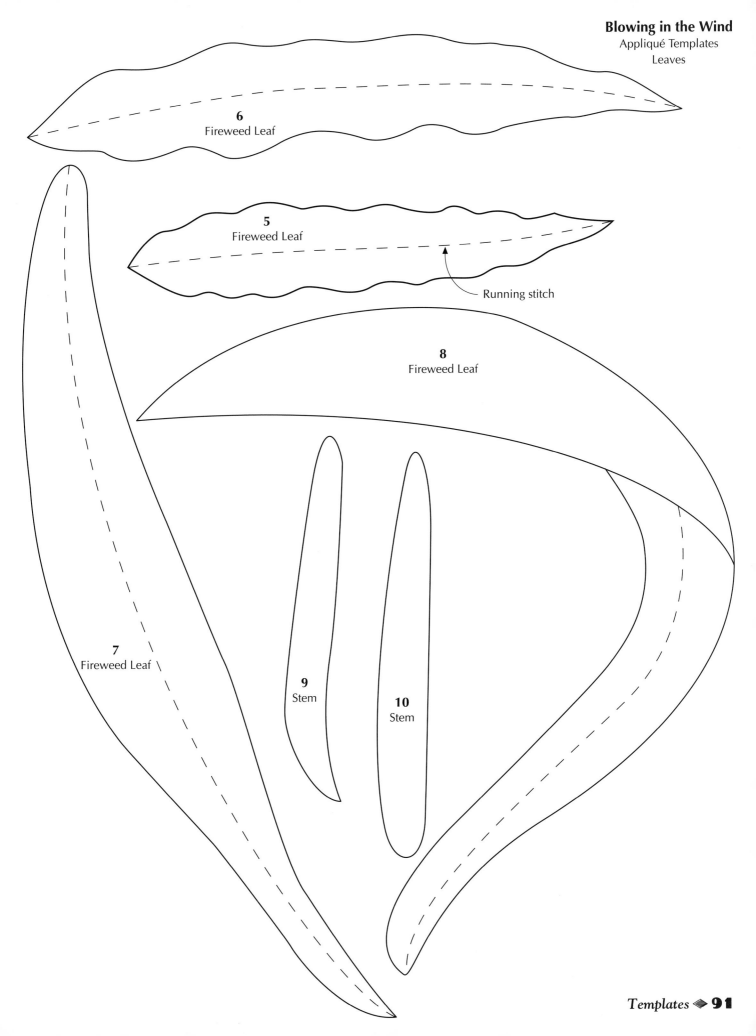

6
Fireweed Leaf

5
Fireweed Leaf

Running stitch

8
Fireweed Leaf

7
Fireweed Leaf

9
Stem

10
Stem

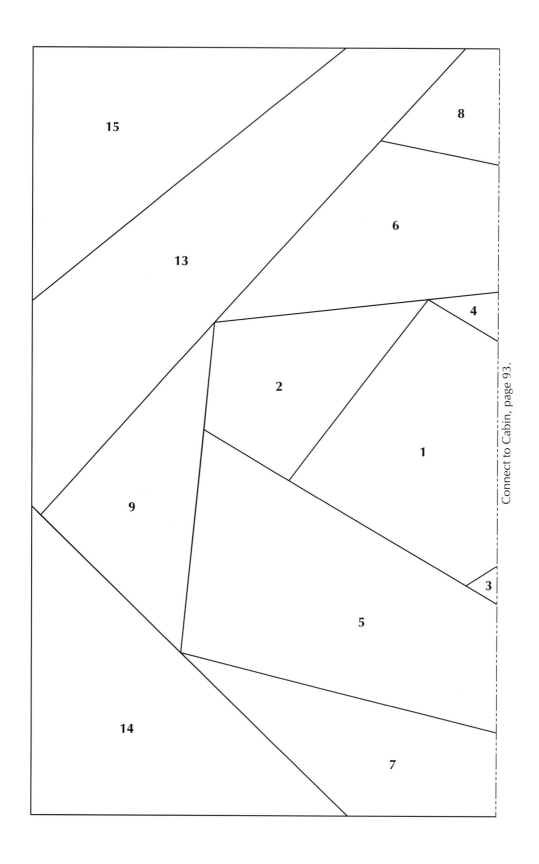

Connect to Cabin, page 93.

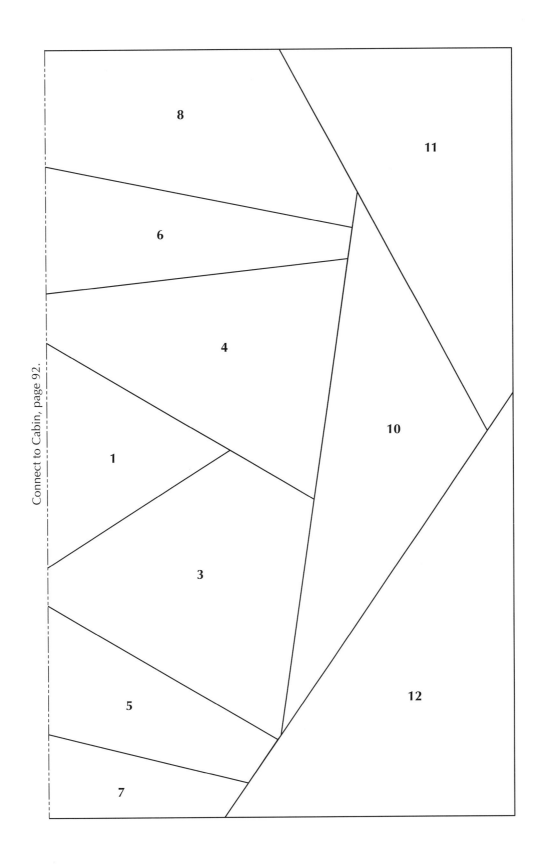

Connect to Cabin, page 92.

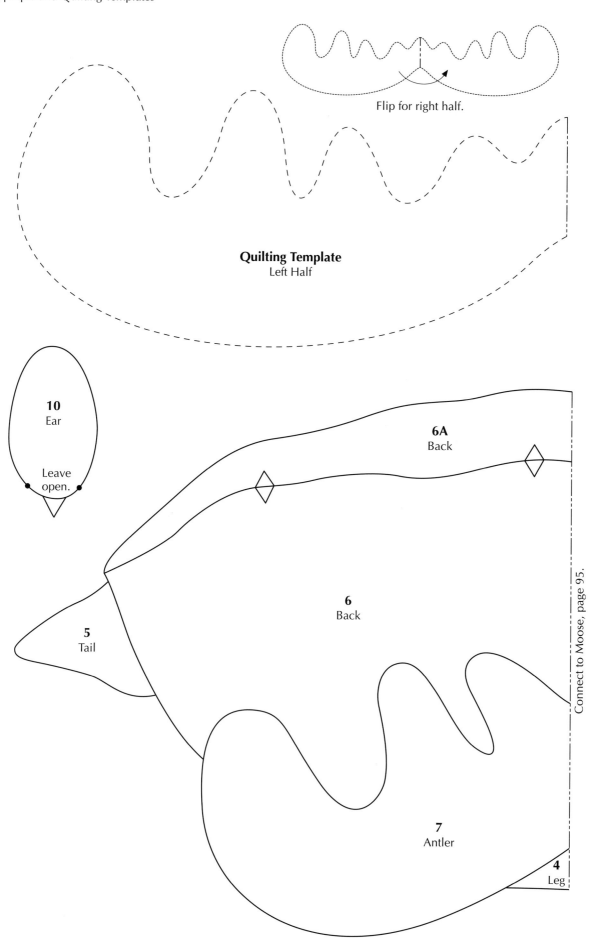

Flip for right half.

Quilting Template
Left Half

10
Ear

Leave
open.

6A
Back

6
Back

5
Tail

7
Antler

4
Leg

Connect to Moose, page 95.

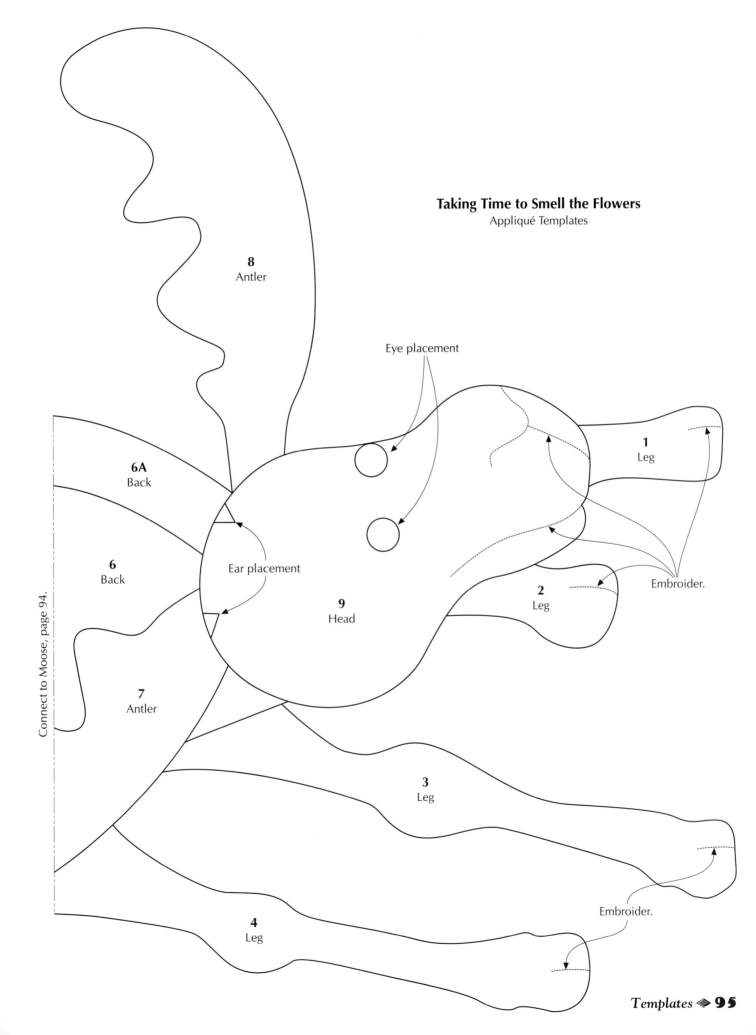

Taking Time to Smell the Flowers
Appliqué Templates

8
Antler

Eye placement

1
Leg

6A
Back

Ear placement

6
Back

2
Leg

Embroider.

9
Head

7
Antler

Connect to Moose, page 94.

3
Leg

4
Leg

Embroider.

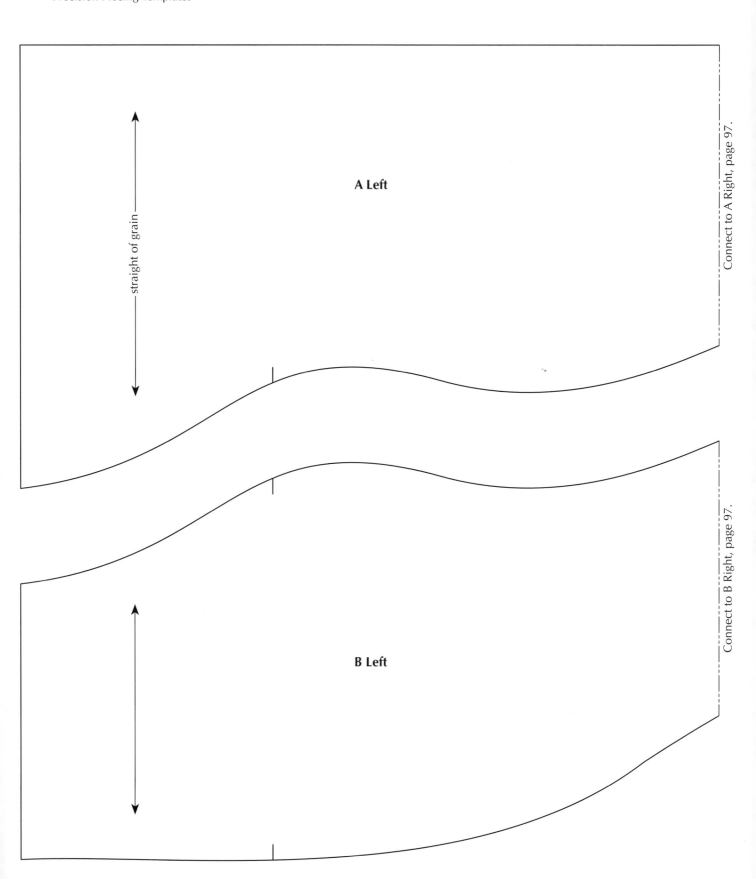

A Left

straight of grain

Connect to A Right, page 97.

Connect to B Right, page 97.

B Left

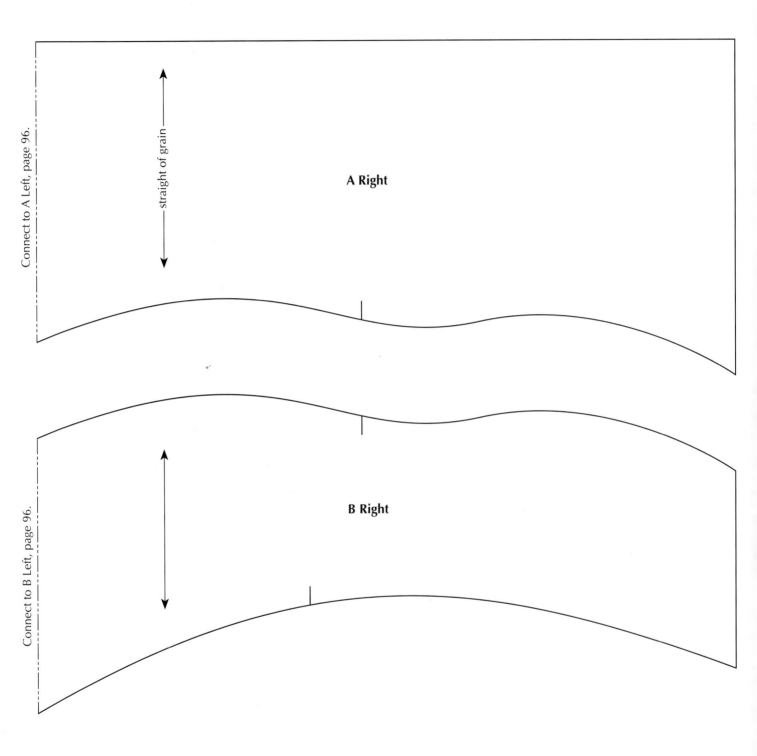

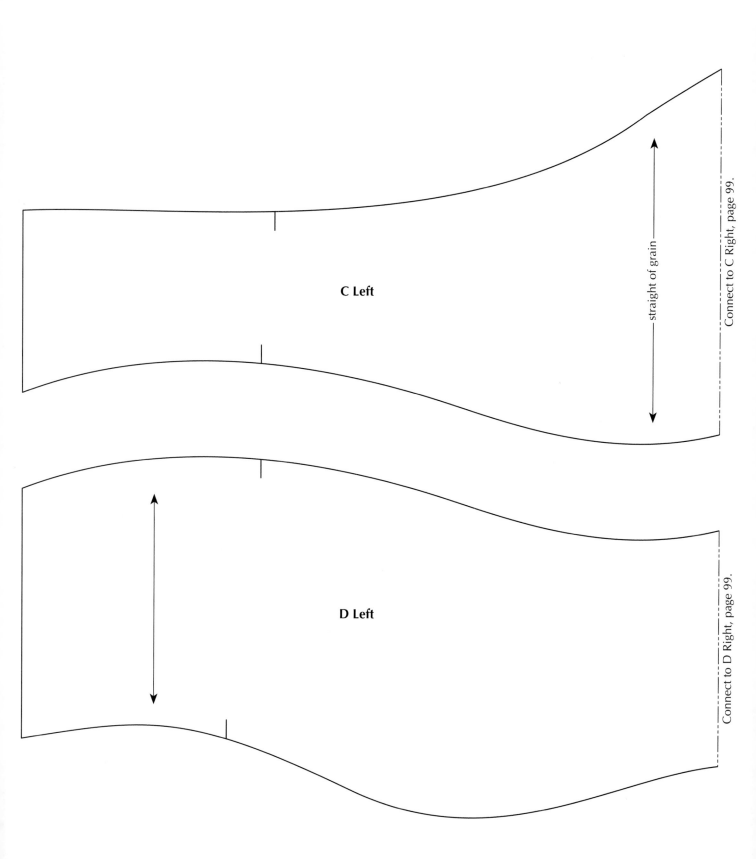

C Left

straight of grain

Connect to C Right, page 99.

D Left

Connect to D Right, page 99.

C Right

Connect to C Left, page 98.

straight of grain

D Right

Connect to D Left, page 98.

Taking Time to Smell the Flowers
Precision Piecing Templates

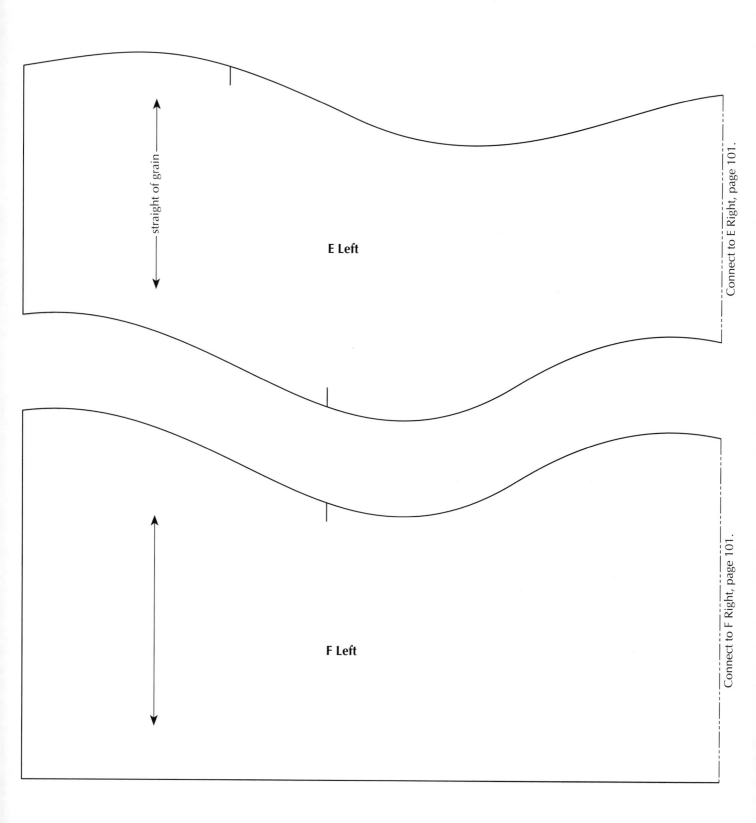

straight of grain

E Left

Connect to E Right, page 101.

F Left

Connect to F Right, page 101.

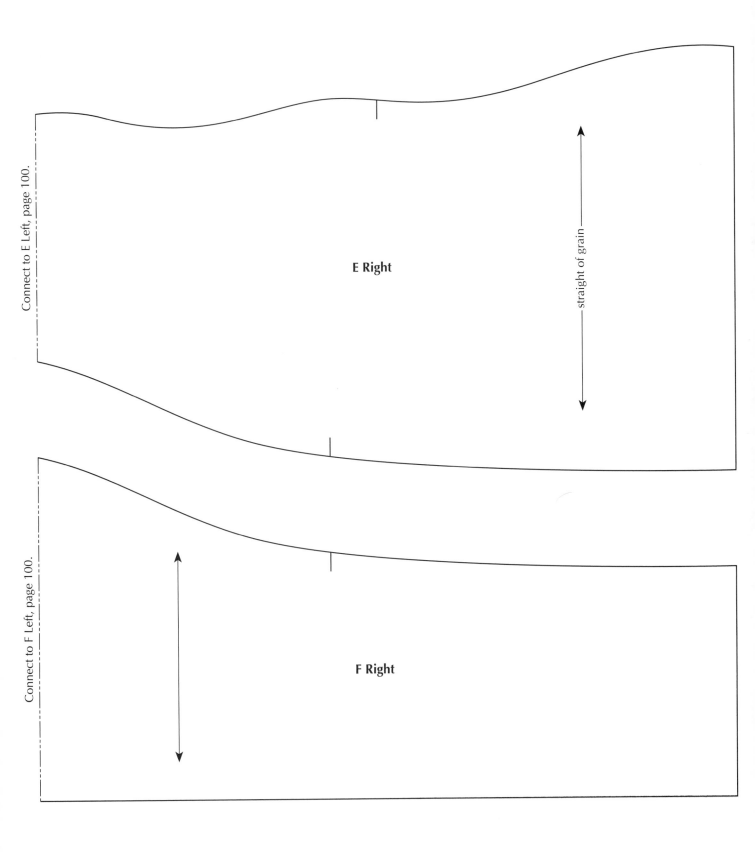

Connect to E Left, page 100.

E Right

straight of grain

Connect to F Left, page 100.

F Right

Quilter's Totem

Appliqué Templates

Templates marked with an *R*
are reverse appliquéd.

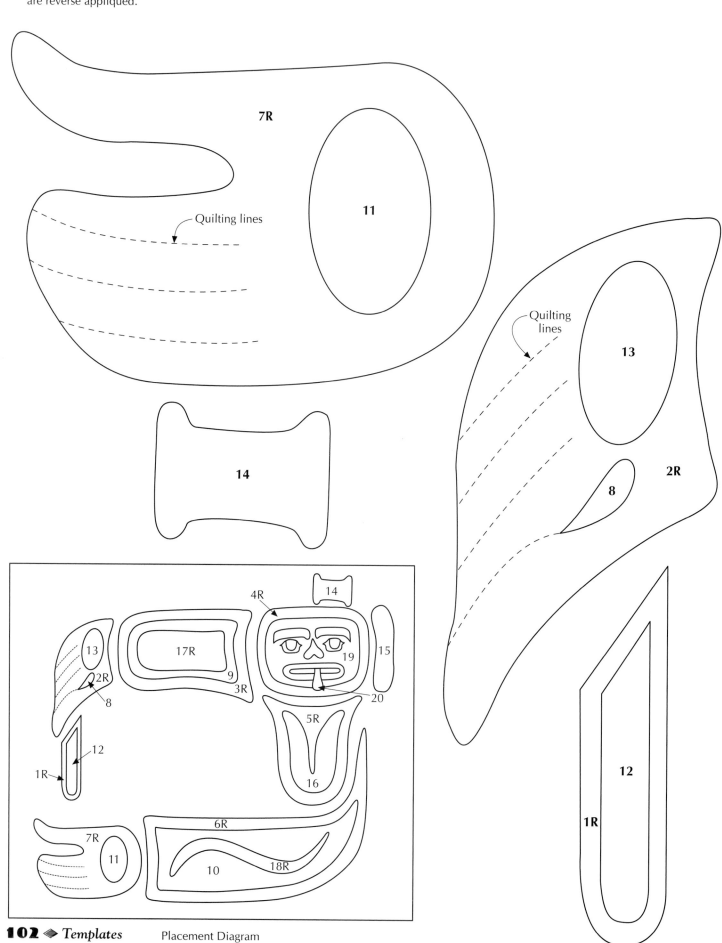

7R

Quilting lines

11

14

Quilting lines

13

2R

8

14

4R

13

17R

2R

8

9

3R

19

15

12

20

1R

5R

16

6R

7R

11

10

18R

12

1R

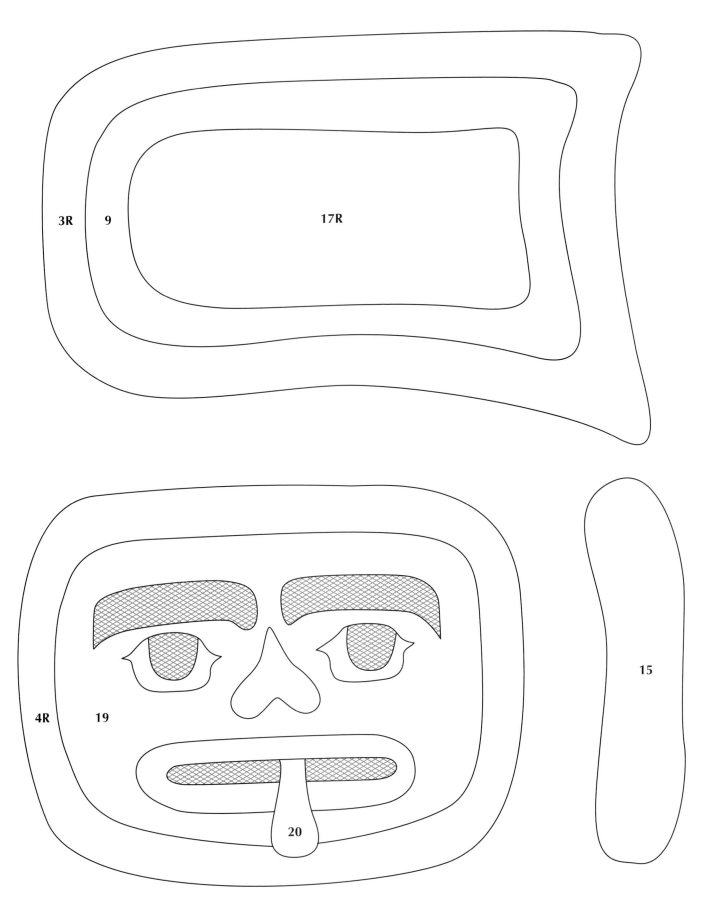

3R 9 17R

4R 19 20 15

Quilter's Totem
Appliqué Templates

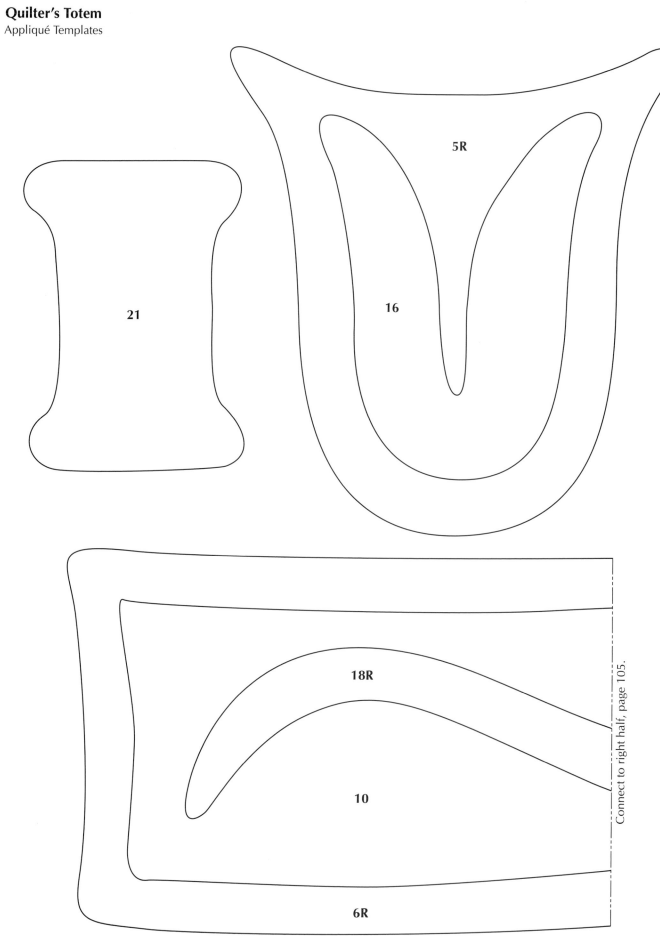

21

5R

16

18R

10

6R

Connect to right half, page 105.

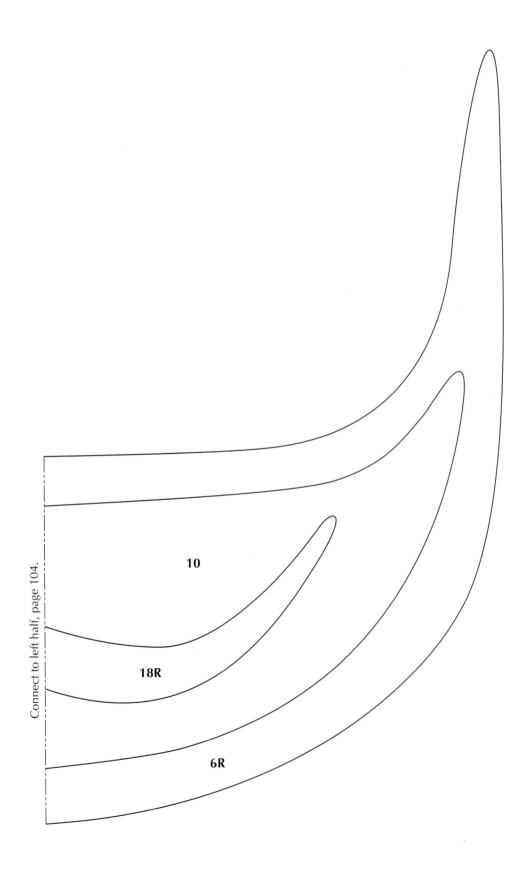

Connect to left half, page 104.

10

18R

6R

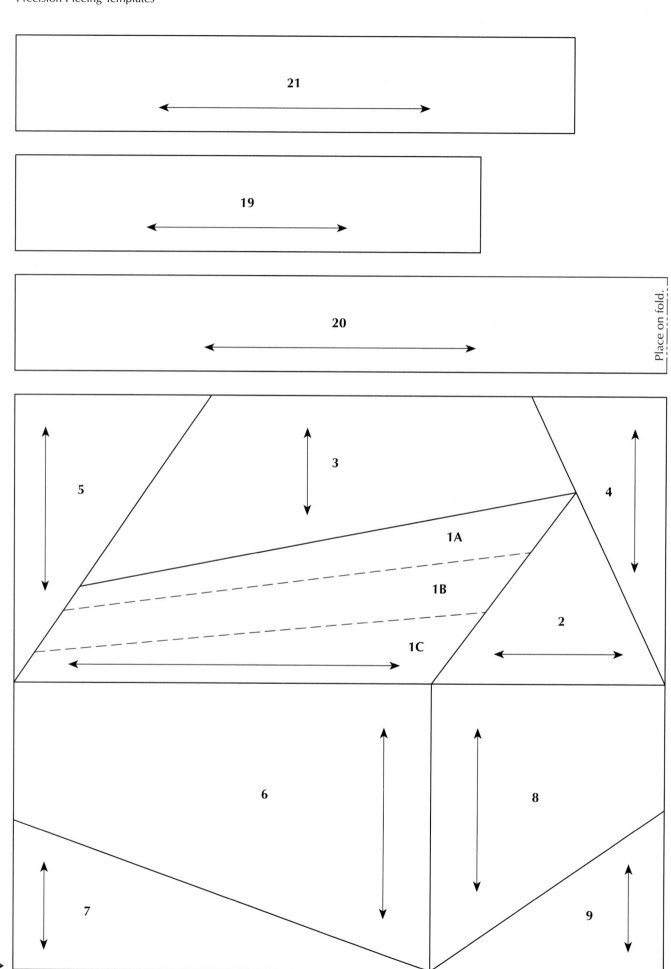

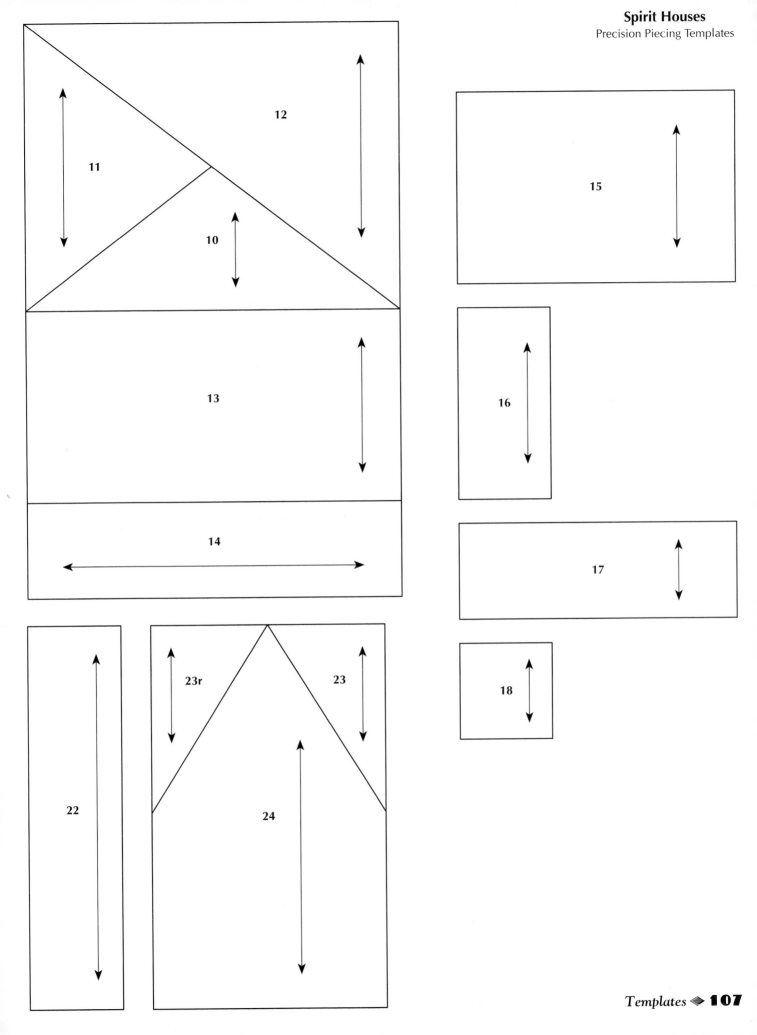

11

12

10

13

14

15

16

17

18

22

23r

23

24

Puffins
Appliqué Templates

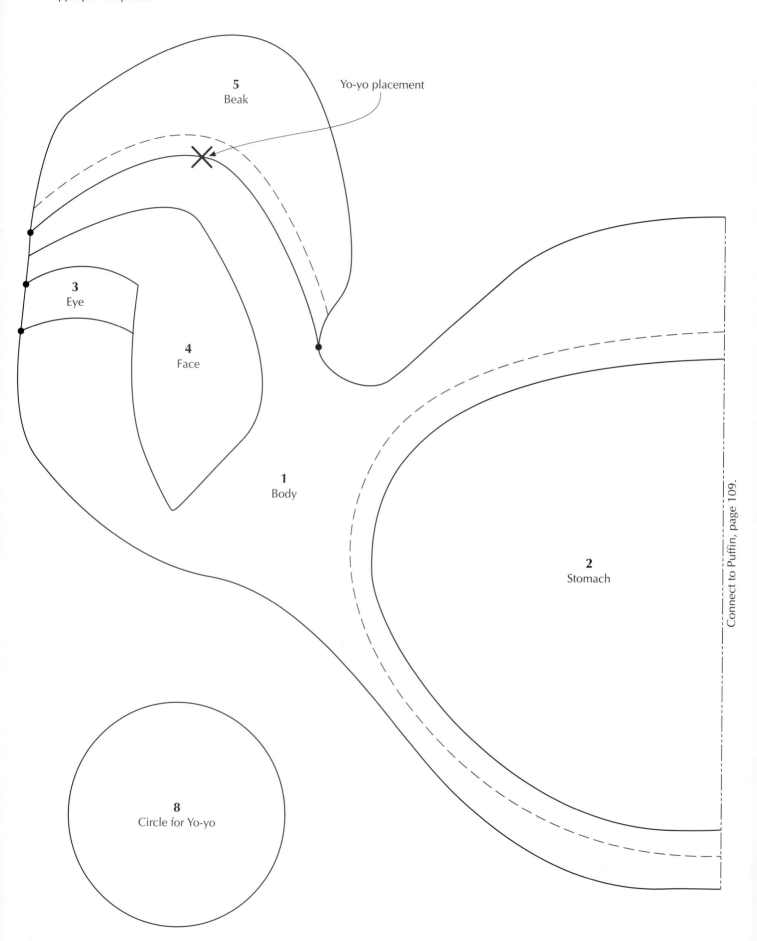

5
Beak

Yo-yo placement

3
Eye

4
Face

1
Body

2
Stomach

Connect to Puffin, page 109.

8
Circle for Yo-yo

Puffins
Appliqué Templates

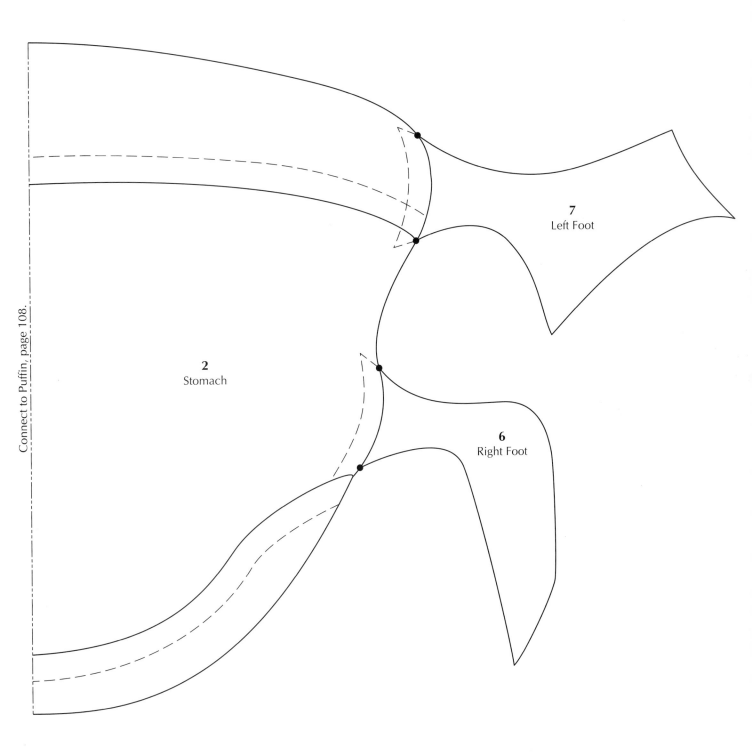

Connect to Puffin, page 108.

2
Stomach

7
Left Foot

6
Right Foot

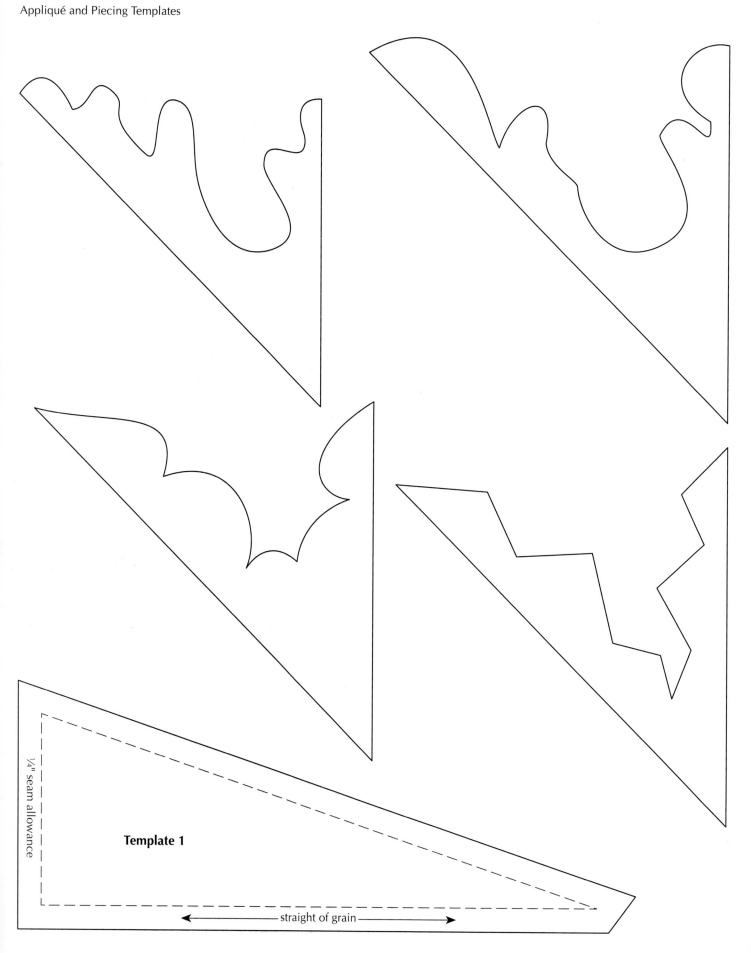

Template 1

¼" seam allowance

straight of grain

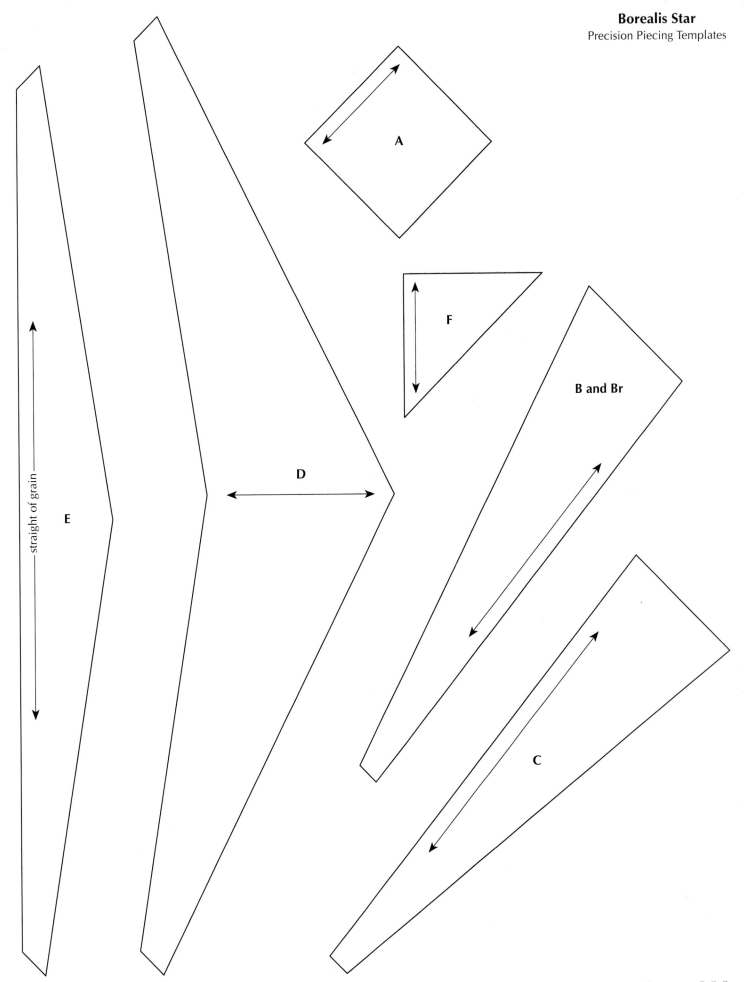

A

F

B and Br

D

straight of grain

E

C

Publications and Products

Many titles are available at your local quilt shop.
For more information, send $2 for a color catalog to
That Patchwork Place, Inc., PO Box 118, Bothell,
WA 98041-0118 USA.

☎ U.S. and Canada, call **1-800-426-3126** for the
name and location of the quilt shop nearest you.
Int'l: 1-206-483-3313   Fax: 1-206-486-7596
E-mail: info@patchwork.com
Web: http://oak.forest.net/patchwork   5.96